The Best of
Just CrossStitch®

Oxmoor House®

The Best of Just CrossStitch

© 1994 by Oxmoor House, Inc.
Book Division of Southern Progress Corporation
P.O. Box 2463, Birmingham, Alabama 35201

Published by Oxmoor House, Inc., Leisure Arts,
Inc., and Symbol of Excellence Publishers, Inc.

Library of Congress Catalog Number: 94-065472
Hardcover ISBN: 0-8487-1164-5
Softcover ISBN: 0-8487-1421-0
Manufactured in the United States of America
First Printing 1994

Oxmoor House, Inc.
Editor-in-Chief: Nancy J. Fitzpatrick
Senior Crafts Editor: Susan Ramey Wright
Copy Editor: Susan Smith Cheatham
Associate Production Manager: Theresa L. Beste
Production Assistant: Marianne Jordan

Symbol of Excellence Publishers, Inc.
Executive Editors: Barbara Cockerham,
Phyllis Hoffman
Editor: Diane Kennedy-Jackson
Editorial Assistants: Susan Branch, Carol Odom,
Carol Zentgraf
Production Manager: Wayne Hoffman
Associate Production Manager: Perry James
Creative Director: Mac Jamieson
Executive Art Director: Yukie McLean
Art Directors: Scott Begley, Michael Whisenant
Graphic Designer: Rick Nance
Photographer: David L. Maxwell
Photography Stylists: Cathy Muir, Ada Parker,
Glenda Parker, Tracey M. Runnion,
Jarinda Wiechman

Dedication

*This book is lovingly dedicated to the memory
of Cathy Ricketts Livingston—
a talented artist, a sister stitcher, and a dear friend.
September 11, 1952-May 9, 1994*

On an autumn day in 1988, Cathy Ricketts Livingston walked into our lives and hearts when she came to interview for a position as a staff artist with *Just CrossStitch*® magazine. After looking at her portfolio, filled to overflowing with wonderful examples of her art, we knew she was a perfect match for the position. We believe Cathy felt the match was perfect, also.

She left a secretarial position in the department of animal science at the University of Tennessee, where she had graduated with honors in 1974 with a fine arts degree, and moved to Birmingham. Cathy adopted the staff at *Just CrossStitch*® as her Alabama family, and settled into her office, surrounded by oil paintings, cross-stitched pieces, and UT pennants.

Creativity seemed to flow from Cathy's fingertips as she designed masterpiece after masterpiece for counted cross stitch. Her artwork is as impressive as her designs for cross stitch, and it is her lifelike renditions of wildlife animals and birds that have made her name synonymous with excellence in design.

Cathy was a talented artist. But more than that, she was a dear friend. Her kindness, caring, and generosity will never be forgotten by those fortunate enough to have known her well.

Always a fighter, Cathy battled cancer for the last three years of her life. While those of us left behind struggle with the loss of our friend, we take comfort from the memories of the time we have shared with Cathy, and in knowing that her legacy will live on forever in stitches.

Introduction

The Best of Just CrossStitch—the title alone implies excellence.

Just CrossStitch® magazine, the first needlework magazine to feature solely counted cross stitch, has earned a reputation with needleworkers as being "the best" when it comes to their number-one hobby—counted cross stitch! Through the years, the magazine has featured the finest work from some of the most talented needlework artists who have ever taken pen to chart paper.

Within the 144 pages of this breathtaking volume is a collection of some of the best designs published throughout the history of *Just CrossStitch*® magazine: gorgeous masterpieces from "The Gallery Collection," heirloom treasures from the "Hope Chest Collection," whimsical, quick-stitch "Coffee Break" designs. You'll find magnificent samplers, charming creations for the younger set, and fabulous holiday stitchery. You're certain to delight in the assortment of projects presented for your stitching enjoyment.

Page 41

We invite you to sit awhile, turn the pages, and select your favorites. Then get ready to enjoy hour after pleasurable hour as you create with needle and floss works of art you'll be proud to call your own.

Happy stitching!

Contents

Page 68

Page 52

Page 9

Editor's Note: *Because this book is a compilation of projects that spans a period of twelve years, some of the fabrics and accessory pieces shown may no longer be available. Contact your local needlework shop owner for suggestions of substitutions that are currently available.*

THE GALLERY COLLECTION

Y ou'll find stunning masterworks of stitchery in "The Gallery Collection." From its inception, early in the history of *Just CrossStitch*® magazine, "The Gallery Collection" has garnered a reputation for featuring stitched works of art. Enthusiastic needle artists will be proud to display these prominently throughout their homes. From simple cross stitch with an elegant look to decorative masterpieces that highlight a host of added stitches, these pieces will challenge even the most skilled needleworker.

Above—*Colonial Fuit Stack,* page 29; Left (clockwise from top left)—*Fruit Bellpull,* page 22; *The Woods,* page 8; *Lily Maiden,* page 35; and *Friends,* page 34.

The Woods

Chart begins on page 10.

Screech Owl

Chart begins on page 13.

Shaded portion indicates overlap from previous page.

THE WOODS

DMC Coats Anchor®

	DMC	Coats	Anchor®	
·	white	1001	01	white
I	762	3068	397	pearl gray, vy. lt.
\	white	1001	01	white
	951	3335	933	flesh, vy. lt.
L	762	8510	397	pearl gray, vy. lt.
	951	3335	933	flesh, vy. lt.
=	415	8510	398	pearl gray
V	415	8510	398	pearl gray
	951	3335	933	flesh, vy. lt.
X	415	8510	398	pearl gray
	402	—	347	mahogany, vy. lt.
Z	415	8510	398	pearl gray
	414	8513	235	steel gray, dk.
6	414	8513	235	steel gray, dk.
M	413	8514	236	pewter gray, dk.
*	413	8514	236	pewter gray, dk.
	310	8403	403	black
■	310	8403	403	black
●	500	6880	879	blue green, vy. dk.
∧	501	6878	878	blue green, dk.
	502	6876	877	blue green
●	502	6876	877	blue green
	3041	4222	871	antique violet, med.
//	3042	4221	869	antique violet, lt.
II	3325	7976	144	baby blue
∪	504	6875	875	blue green, lt.
	3325	7976	144	baby blue
▲	3011	—	845	khaki, dk.
W	3012	—	844	khaki, med.
◣	3371	5478	382	black-brown
3	938	5477	381	coffee, ul. dk.
+	3031	5472	381	mocha, vy. dk.
o	433	5471	944	brown, med.
⌐	434	5000	370	brown, lt.
N	3371	5478	382	black-brown
	413	8514	236	pewter gray, dk.
/	3325	7976	144	baby blue (half cross)
ss	890	6021	212	pistachio, ul. dk.
	367	6018	210	pistachio, dk.
ss	319	6246	246	pistachio, vy. dk.

Fabric: 32-count raw Belfast linen from Zweigart®
Stitch count: 142H x119W
Design size:
14-count 10⅛" x 8½"
18-count 7⅞" x 6⅝"
27-count 10½" x 8⅞"
32-count 8⅞" x 7⅜"

Instructions: Cross stitch over two threads, using two strands of floss. Back-stitch using one strand of floss unless otherwise indicated. Make French knots using two strands white/1001/01 for dot in eye of each chickadee, wrapping floss around needle once. Straight stitch using one strand of floss unless otherwise in-

(Continued on the next page)

(The Woods continued)
dicated. When two colors are bracketed together, use one strand of each. Use alphabet and numerals to personalize.

Backstitch instructions:

938	5477	381	lettering (two strands)
890	6021	212	initials and date (two strands)
3371	5478	382	pinecones
3031	5472	381	branch under large chickadee
413	8514	236	birds flying over mountains, both beaks on chickadees, legs on large chickadee
310	8403	403	black caps and throats on both chickadees
762	3068	397	lines over both chickadees' eyes
415	8510	398	lines in wing of small chickadee, lines in tail of large chickadee
414	8513	235	remainder of each chickadee

Straight stitch (ss) instructions:

⌐890	6021	212	pine needles in border
└367	6018	210	(one strand of each)
319	6246	246	pine needles from branches
367	6018	210	pine needles from branches (one strand, stitch **over** 319/6246/246)

Designed by Cathy Livingston

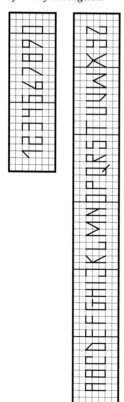

SCREECH OWL

DMC Coats Anchor®

	DMC	Coats	Anchor	
✱	801	5475	353	coffee, dk.
ε	433	5471	944	brown, med.
∧	⌐434	5000	370	brown, lt.
	└435	5371	363	brown, vy. lt.
⌐	⌐436	5943	362	tan
	└437	5942	361	tan, lt.
//	⌐739	5369	942	tan, ul. lt.
	└712	5387	926	cream
e	⌐3782	—	831	mocha brown, lt.
	└712	5387	926	cream
✗	⌐801	5475	353	coffee, dk.
	└356	2975	9575	terra cotta, med.
Z	⌐758	3868	868	terra cotta, lt.
	└356	2975	9575	terra cotta, med.
◗	758	3868	868	terra cotta, lt.
T	948	2331	778	peach flesh, vy. lt.
≠	950	2336	376	flesh, lt.
Y	407	—	883	flesh, dk.
•	white	1001	01	white
■	310	8403	403	black
6	844	8501	382	beaver gray, ul. dk.
X	⌐645	8500	273	beaver gray, vy. dk.
	└610	5889	889	drab brown, vy. dk.
C	⌐647	8900	8581	beaver gray, med.
	└612	—	832	drab brown, med.
∠	680	2876	907	old gold, dk.
4	⌐680	2876	907	old gold, dk.
	└783	5307	307	gold
△	783	5307	307	gold
U	725	2298	305	topaz
‖‖	726	2295	295	topaz, lt.
●	⌐890	6021	212	pistachio, ul. dk.
	└938	5477	381	coffee, ul. dk.
▼	⌐367	6018	210	pistachio, dk.
	└890	6021	212	pistachio, ul. dk.
а	647	8900	8581	beaver gray, med.
▲	938	5477	381	coffee, ul. dk.
3	⌐938	5477	381	coffee, ul. dk.
	└300	—	352	mahogany, vy. dk.
+	300	—	352	mahogany, vy. dk.
∟	400	—	351	mahogany, dk.
◖	⌐844	8501	382	beaver gray, ul. dk.
	└938	5477	381	coffee, ul. dk.
>	⌐938	5477	381	coffee, ul. dk.
	└640	5393	393	beige-gray, vy. dk.
N	⌐938	5477	381	coffee, ul. dk.
	└3782	—	831	mocha brown, lt.
J	⌐640	5393	393	beige-gray, vy. dk.
	└3776	—	349	mahogany, lt.
W	⌐3776	—	349	mahogany, lt.
	└3782	—	831	mocha brown, lt.
o	⌐640	5393	393	beige-gray, vy. dk.
	└543	5533	376	beige-brown, ul. lt.
⌒	⌐3782	—	831	mocha brown, lt.
	└543	5533	376	beige-brown, ul. lt.
∕	⌐white	1001	01	white
	└543	5533	376	biege-brown, lt.
⊙	⌐647	8900	8581	beaver gray, med.
	└3782	—	831	mocha brown, lt.
⦀	⌐400	—	351	mahogany, dk.
	└640	5393	393	beige-gray, vy. dk.
ss	319	6246	246	pistachio, vy. dk.

Fabric: 28-count antique green linen from Wichelt Imports, Inc.
Stitch count: 140H x 90W
Design size:
14-count 10" x 6½"
18-count 7¾" x 5"
25-count 11¼" x 7¼"
28-count 10" x 6½"

Instructions: Cross stitch over two threads, using two strands of floss. Backstitch using one strand of floss. Make French knot in owl's eye where ● appears at intersecting grid lines, using two strands white/1001/01 and wrapping floss around needle once. Make straight stitches using one strand of floss. When two colors are bracketed together, use one strand of each.

Backstitch instructions:
Backstitch in order listed.

844	8501	382	beak
310	8403	403	center of eyes
938	5477	381	yellow area of eyes, eyebrows
640	5393	393	base of right ear and down right side to first ● on right edge of breast
543	5533	376	from first ● on right edge of breast around to mouse's ear
801	5475	353	ears, eye, forehead to nose, lower back to mouse's tail
407	—	883	remainder of mouse
938	5477	381	remainder of owl
844	8501	382	pine branches

Straight stitch (ss) instructions:

890	6021	212	pine needles
319	6246	246	repeat on top of 890/6021/212 for pine needles
3782	—	831	mouse's whiskers
543	5533	376	feathers over owl's beak

Designed by Cathy Livingston

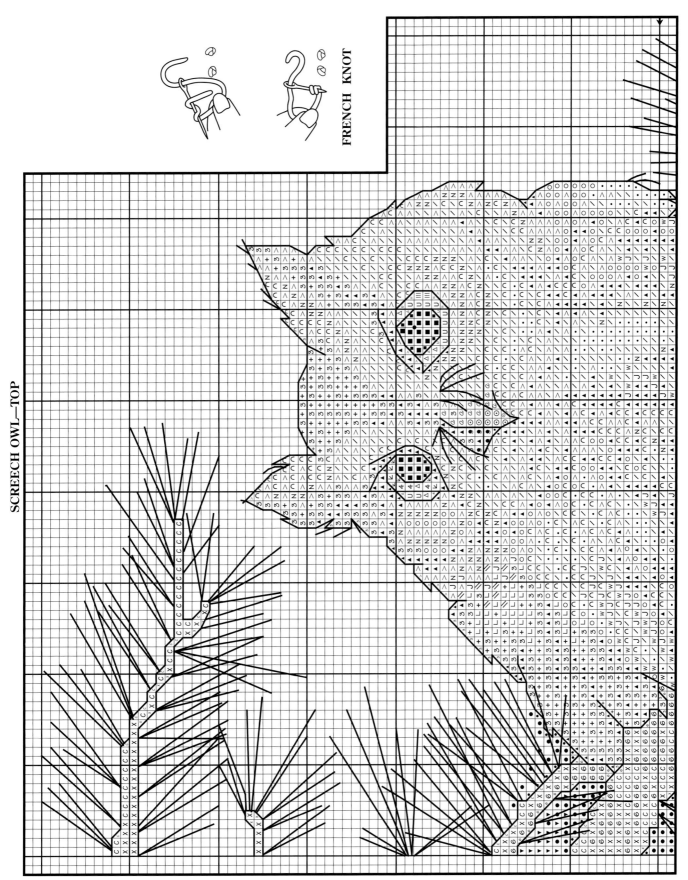

SCREECH OWL—TOP

FRENCH KNOT

(Continued on the next page)

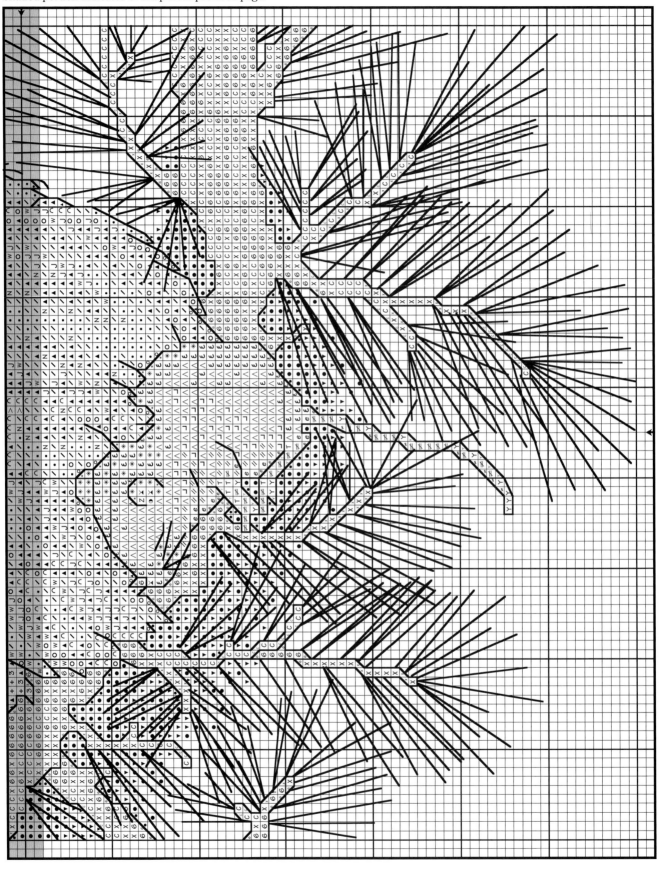

14

Gentlemen's Gathering

Chart begins on page 16.

GENTLEMEN'S GATHERING

	DMC	Coats	Anchor®	
●	310	8403	403	black
−	white	1001	01	white
Z	347	3013	13	salmon, dk.
L	3328	3071	10	salmon, med.
∴	402	—	347	mahogany, vy. lt.
·	951	3335	933	sportsman flesh, vy. lt.
‖	ecru	1002	387	ecru
T	317	8512	400	pewter gray
J	318	8511	399	steel gray, lt.
⌐	762	8510	397	pearl gray, vy. lt.
X	975	5349	355	golden brown, dk.
H	801	5475	353	coffee brown, dk.
O	433	5471	944	brown, med.
C	435	5371	363	brown, vy. lt.
╱	676	2874	887	old gold, lt.
:	647	8900	8581	beaver gray, med.
╱╱	646	8500	273	beaver gray, dk.
✳	645	5800	273	beaver gray, vy. dk.
3	3012	6843	844	khaki green, med.
□	3013	6842	842	khaki green, lt.
N	3011	6845	845	khaki green, dk.
S	3072	2292	234	beaver gray, vy. lt.
∧	747	7053	928	sky blue, vy. lt.
e	739	5369	942	tan, ul. lt.
⌐	738	5375	372	tan, vy. lt.
+	922	3336	347	copper, lt.
∩	680	2876	907	old gold, dk.
Φ	744	2293	301	yellow, pl.
bs	938	5477	381	coffee brown, ul. dk.

Fabric: 14-count Victorian green Aida from Zweigart®

Stitch count: 164H x 164W

Design size:
14-count   11¾" x 11¾"
18-count   9⅛" x 9⅛"
22-count   7½" x 7½"
32-count   10¼" x 10¼"

Instructions: Cross stitch using three strands of floss. Backstitch using two strands of floss.

Backstitch (bs) instructions:
647 8900 8581   blades of grass
938 5477 381   horses' bridles
310 8403 403   remainder of backstitching

Designed by Linda Gordanier Jary

Water Lilies

	DMC	Coats	Anchor®	
·	white	1001	01	white
=	415	8393	398	pearl gray
⁄	818	3281	23	baby pink
C[	3326	3126	36	rose, lt.
	415	8398	398	pearl gray
M[	335	3283	38	rose
	318	8511	399	steel gray, lt.
⊙	727	2289	293	topaz, vy. lt.
+	725	2298	305	topaz
Z[	977	2306	313	gold brown, lt.
	725	2298	305	topaz
●[	938	5477	381	coffee, ul. dk.
	221	3242	897	pink, dk.
W	221	3242	897	pink, dk.
	3722	—	896	pink, med.
ε[	3721	—	—	pink, dk.
	3722	—	896	pink, med.
L[	3012	6843	844	khaki, med.
	3722	—	896	pink, med.
II[	3013	6842	842	khaki, lt.
	223	3241	895	pink, med.
-	3013	6842	842	khaki, lt.
*[	890	6021	212	pistachio, ul. dk.
	934	6270	862	avocado-black
4[	367	6018	210	pistachio, dk.
	319	6246	246	pistachio, vy. dk.
3	367	6018	210	pistachio, dk. (three skeins)
X	320	6017	215	pistachio, med.
V	368	6016	214	pistachio, lt.
╲	369	6015	260	pistachio, vy. lt.
5	934	6270	862	avocado-black
⑊[	834	—	945	olive, vy. lt.
	3013	6842	842	khaki, lt.
>[	3013	6842	842	khaki, lt.
	368	6016	214	pistachio, lt.
6[	3012	6843	844	khaki, med.
	320	6017	215	pistachio, med.
⌐	834	—	945	olive, vy. lt.
■[	310	8403	403	black
	823	7982	150	navy, dk. (two skeins)
▲[	890	6021	212	pistachio, ul. dk.
	823	7982	150	navy, dk.
●[	319	6246	246	pistachio, vy. dk.
	336	7981	150	navy
★[	890	6021	212	pistachio, ul. dk.
	830	—	277	olive, dk.
N	830	—	277	olive, dk.
⁄⁄[	833	—	374	olive, lt.
	831	—	277	olive, med.
⌐[	801	5475	353	coffee, dk.
	830	—	277	olive, dk.

Fabric: 32-count sage Jobelan from Wichelt Imports, Inc.
Stitch count: 98H x 156W
Design size:
14-count 7" x 11¼"
18-count 5½" x 8⅝"
32-count 6⅛" x 9¾"

Instructions: Cross stitch over two threads, using two strands of floss. When two colors are bracketed together, use one strand of each.

Designed by Cathy Livingston

Chart begins on page 20.

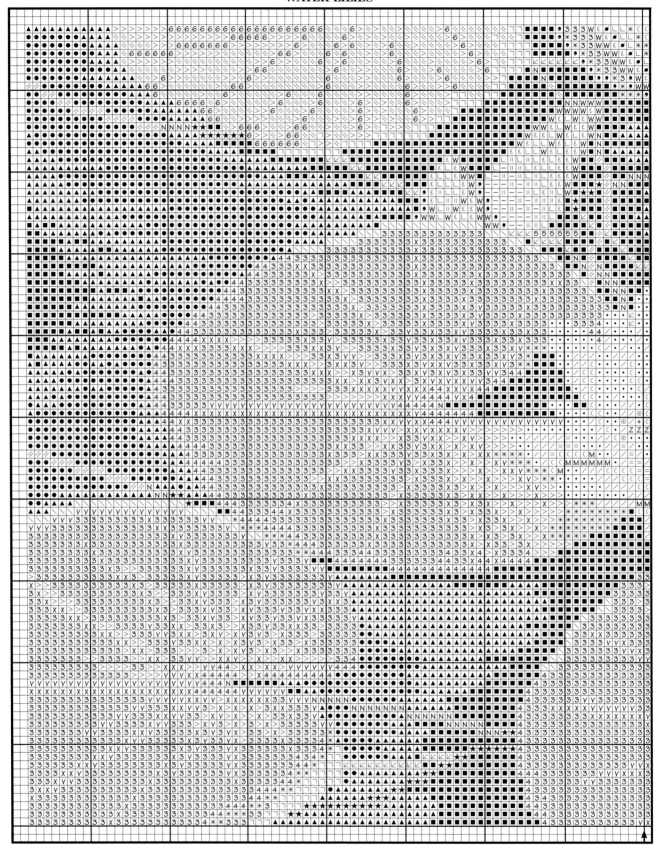

Shaded portion indicates overlap from previous page.

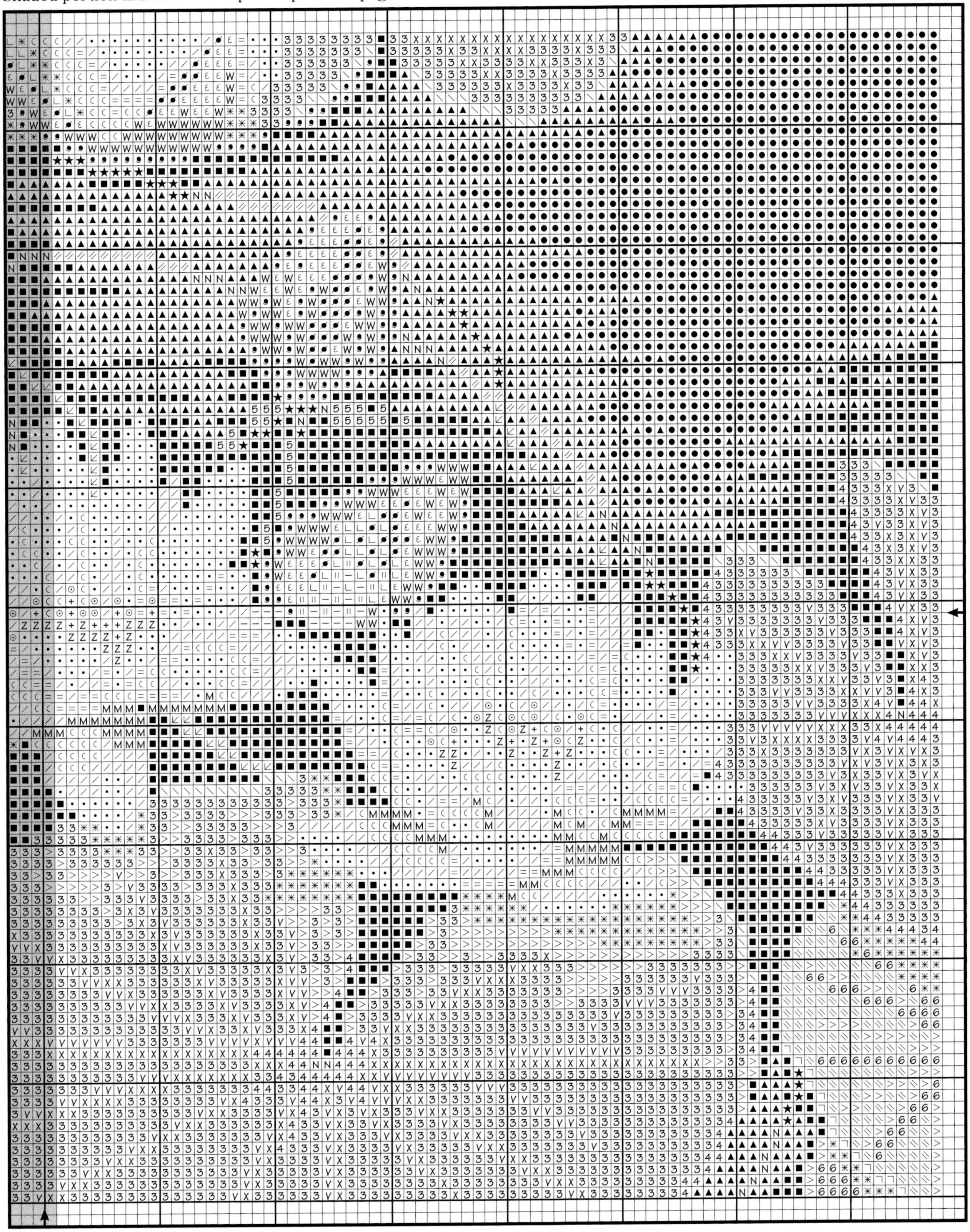

Fruit
Bellpull

DMC	Coats	Anchor®	
•	3046	2410	888	yellow-beige, med.
♡	422	5372	942	hazelnut, lt.
=	3045	2412	886	yellow-beige, dk.
X	3045	2412	886	yellow-beige, dk.
	610	5889	889	drab brown, vy. dk.
▽	3047	2300	956	yellow-beige, lt.
	950	2336	376	flesh, lt.
∩	3046	2410	888	yellow-beige, med.
	3773	2337	882	flesh, med.
◁	422	5372	942	hazelnut, lt.
	3064	3883	379	flesh, med.
⊥	3046	2410	888	yellow-beige, med.
	3013	6842	842	khaki, lt.
μ	422	5372	942	hazelnut, lt.
	3013	6842	842	khaki, lt.
8	3045	2412	886	yellow-beige, dk.
	3012	6843	844	khaki, med.
c	613	—	956	drab brown, lt.
	3047	2300	956	yellow-beige, lt.
⌐	372	—	853	mustard, lt.
	422	5372	942	hazelnut, lt.
◁	371	—	854	mustard
	3045	2412	886	yellow-beige, dk.
∧	224	3240	894	pink, lt.
	758	3868	868	terra cotta, lt.
+	223	3241	895	pink, med.
	3778	2338	9575	terra cotta, lt.
3	3722	5579	896	pink, med.
	356	2975	9575	terra cotta, med.
M	221	3242	897	pink, dk.
	400	5349	351	mahogany, dk.
◇	3773	2337	882	flesh, med.
	758	3868	868	terra cotta, lt.
//	3064	3883	379	flesh, med.
	3778	2338	9575	terra cotta, lt.
◥	3772	5579	379	flesh, dk.
	356	2975	9575	terra cotta, med.
ℓ	950	2336	376	flesh, lt.
	437	5942	361	tan, lt.
Z	3773	2337	882	flesh, med.
	436	5943	362	tan
∴	3064	3883	379	flesh, med.
	435	5371	363	brown, vy. lt.
6	316	3081	969	mauve, med.
	3722	3241	896	pink, med.

PEACHES

4	3726	3084	970	mauve, med. lt.
	3721	3242	896	pink, dk.
ɕ	315	3082	972	mauve, dk.
	221	3242	897	pink, dk.
◤	315	3082	972	mauve, dk.
	3041	4222	871	antique violet, med.
⊐	950	2336	376	flesh, lt.
	3743	4220	869	antique violet, vy. lt.
♂	3773	2337	1008	flesh, med.
	3042	4221	869	antique violet, lt.
$	3064	3883	379	flesh, med.
	3042	4221	869	antique violet, lt.

★	3772	5579	379	flesh, dk.
	3041	4222	871	antique violet, med.
∪	316	3081	969	mauve, med.
	3042	4221	869	antique violet, lt.
⊗	3726	3084	970	mauve, med. lt.
	3041	4222	871	antique violet, med.
♦	315	3082	972	mauve, dk.
	3740	4223	872	antique violet, dk.
∙∙	223	3241	895	pink, med.
E	3722	3241	896	pink, med.
V	3721	3242	896	pink, dk.
&	221	3242	897	pink, dk.

(Continued on the next page)

Shaded portion indicates overlap from previous page.

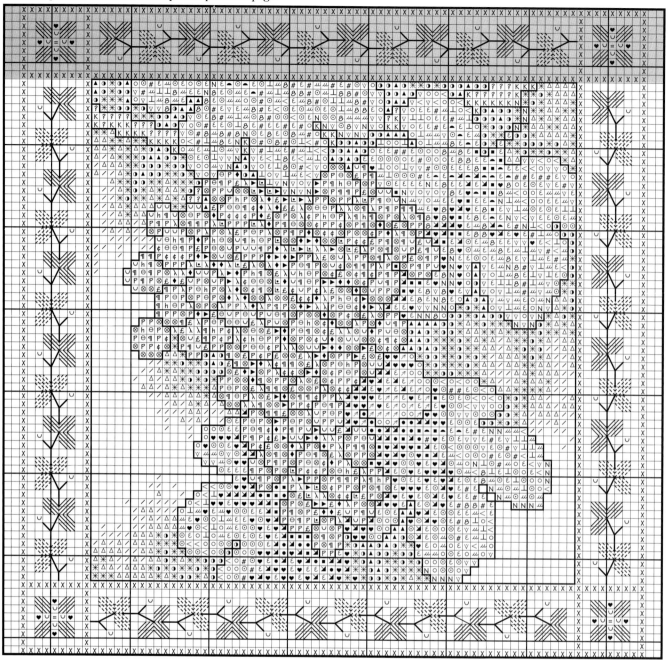

GRAPES

⊖	223	3241	895	pink, med.
	316	3081	969	mauve, med.
‖	3721	3242	896	pink, dk.
	3726	3084	970	mauve, med. lt.
λ	315	3082	972	mauve, dk.
φ	814	3044	44	garnet, dk.
⊡	902	3083	897	garnet, vy. dk.
⍺	224	3240	894	pink, lt.
	3773	2337	822	flesh, med.
↗	223	3241	895	pink, med.
	3064	3883	379	flesh, med.
≠	3722	3241	896	pink, med.
	3772	5579	379	flesh, dk.

▶	221	3242	897	pink, dk.
	632	5936	936	coffee brown, dk.
⌐	3743	4220	869	antique violet, vy. lt.
	3747	7004	120	blue-violet, vy. lt.
∧	3042	4221	869	antique violet, lt.
	341	7005	117	blue-violet, lt.
∞	3041	4222	871	antique violet, med.
	340	7110	118	blue-violet, med.
✕	3740	4223	872	antique violet, dk.
	3746	—	1030	blue-violet, dk.
∴	3743	4220	869	antique violet, vy. lt.
	778	3060	968	mauve, lt.

Shaded portion indicates overlap from previous page.

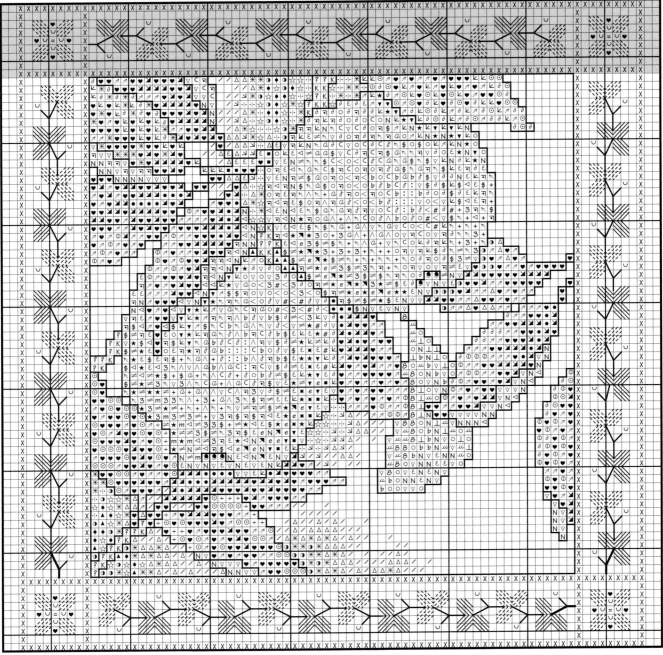

APPLES

: [	822	5830	830 beige-gray, lt.
	712	5387	926 cream
e [	632	5936	936 coffee brown, dk.
	3740	4223	872 antique violet, dk.
↘	503	6879	876 blue-green, med.
·|·	502	6876	877 blue-green
☆	501	6878	878 blue-green, dk.
◆	500	6880	879 blue-green, vy. dk.
∕	524	6315	858 fern green, vy. lt.
△	503	6879	876 blue-green, med.
* [	502	6876	877 blue-green
	3363	6317	262 pine green, med.

◖ [	501	6878	878 blue-green, dk.
	3362	6318	269 pine green, dk.
▲ [	500	6880	879 blue-green, vy. dk.
	520	6318	862 fern green, dk.
÷ [	524	6315	858 fern green, vy. lt.
	3364	6317	262 pine green, med.
⊙ [	523	6316	859 fern green, lt.
	3363	6317	262 pine green, med.
♥	3363	6317	262 pine green, med.
◤	3362	6318	269 pine green, dk.
●	520	6318	862 fern green, dk.
Φ	3053	6315	860 green-gray

(Continued on the next page)

Shaded portion indicates overlap from previous page.

PEARS

↗	522	6316	860	fern green	▼	3362	6318	269	pine green, dk.
✕	3051	6317	846	green-gray, dk.		3011	6845	845	khaki, dk.
<	3013	6842	842	khaki, lt.	○	3013	6842	842	khaki, lt.
	3348	6266	264	yellow-green, lt.	ε	3012	6843	844	khaki, med.
#	3012	6843	844	khaki, med.	■	3011	6845	845	khaki, dk.
	3347	6266	264	yellow-green, med.	♭	613	—	956	drab brown, lt.
◖	3011	6845	845	khaki, dk.	∨	372	—	853	mustard, lt.
	3346	6258	268	hunter	N	371	—	854	mustard
∂	3053	6315	860	green-gray	◑	370	—	855	mustard, med.
	3013	6842	842	khaki, lt.	∪	3032	5393	903	mocha, med.
↙	522	6316	860	fern green	◕	3790	5393	393	beige-gray, ul. dk.
	3012	6843	844	khaki, med.	>	612	—	832	drab brown, med.

Shaded portion indicates overlap from previous page.

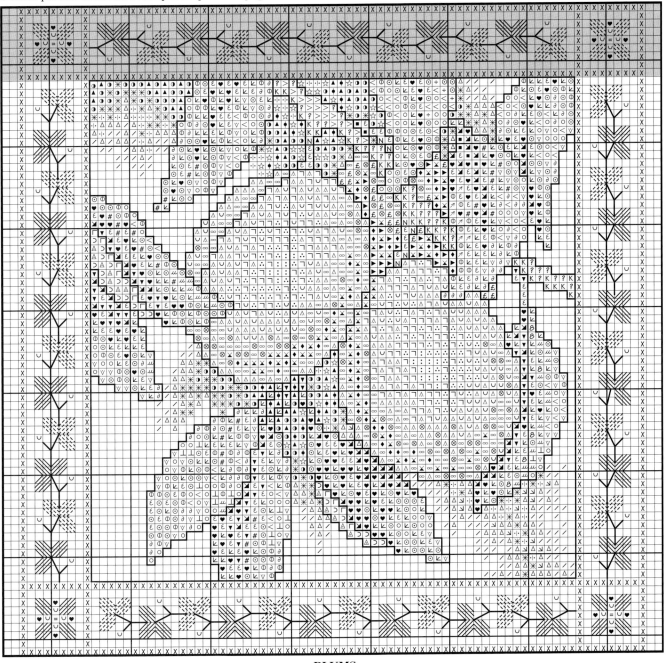

PLUMS

?	611	5898	898	drab brown, dk.
K	610	5889	889	drab brown, vy. dk.
¶	316	3081	969	mauve, med.
P	3726	3084	970	mauve, med. lt.
⌈	613	—	956	drab brown, lt.
⌊	524	6315	858	fern green, vy. lt.
⊃⌈	372	—	853	mustard, lt.
⌊	523	6316	859	fern green, lt.
Δ⌈	371	—	854	mustard
⌊	3052	6316	860	green-gray, med.
h	225	3239	892	pink, vy. lt.
¢	3042	4221	871	antique violet, lt.
£	3041	4222	871	antique violet, med.

►	3740	4223	872	antique violet, dk.
bs	838	5381	380	beige-brown, vy. dk.
bs	3021	5395	273	brown-gray, dk.

Fabric: 28-count bone Brittney from Zweigart® (Cut fabric 38" x 13⅓".)
Stitch count: 429H x 79W
Design size:
25-count 34⅜" x 6⅜"
28-count 30⅝" x 5⅝"
30-count 28⅝" x 5¼"
32-count 26⅞" x 5"

(Continued on the next page)

Shaded portion indicates overlap from previous page.

CHERRIES

NOTE: Please read instructions carefully before beginning. Color code is for entire project. Some symbols may not appear in every chart.

Instructions: Cross stitch over two threads, using two strands of floss. Backstitch using one strand of floss. Satin stitch leaves in border, making stitches in the direction of lines on chart. When two colors are bracketed together, use one strand of each.

Backstitch (bs) instructions:

610	5889	889	inner edge of borders, apples, pears, peaches
3790	5393	393	stems of plum tree, stems of cherry tree

3740	4223	872	plums
838	5381	380	cherries
370	—	855	two lightest leaves in pear block, lighter leaf in apple block, all leaves in plum block, all leaves in grape block
520	6318	862	remainder of leaves
3021	5395	273	grapes, branches
3362	6318	269	vines in border

Satin stitch instructions:

⌐ 3363	6317	262	leaves in border
⌊ 3052	6316	860	
⌐ 3362	6318	269	leaves in border
⌊ 3051	6317	846	

Designed by Teresa Wentzler

Colonial Fruit Stack

Charts begin on page 30.

COLONIAL FRUIT STACK

DMC Coats Anchor®

symbol	DMC	Coats	Anchor	color
■	3371	5478	382	black-brown
●	898	5476	360	coffee brown, vy. dk.
≠	433	5471	944	brown, med.
⊃	435	5371	363	brown, vy. lt. (half cross)
▲	934	6270	862	avocado-black
W	936	6269	269	avocado, vy. dk.
ℓ	937	6268	268	avocado, med.
\	470	6010	267	avocado, lt.
•⌈	895	6021	246	green, dk.
⌊	3371	5478	382	black-brown
N⌈	367	6018	210	pistachio, dk.
⌊	319	6246	246	pistachio, vy. dk.
–	320	6017	215	pistachio, med.
▼⌈	3777	—	—	terra cotta. vy. dk.
⌊	898	5476	360	coffee brown, vy. dk.
✳	3777	—	—	terra cotta, vy. dk.
3⌈	3777	—	—	terra cotta, vy. dk.
⌊	349	2335	13	coral, dk.
+⌈	3777	—	—	terra cotta, vy. dk.
⌊	350	3111	11	coral, med.
○⌈	350	3111	11	coral, med.
⌊	720	2322	236	spice, dk.
=⌈	356	2975	9575	terra cotta, med.
⌊	721	2324	324	spice, med.
∴⌈	356	2975	9575	terra cotta, med.
⌊	3774	—	778	flesh, vy. lt.
ʟ	349	2335	13	coral, dk.
⊙⌈	349	2335	13	coral, dk.
⌊	783	5307	307	gold
>⌈	350	3111	11	coral, med.
⌊	725	2298	305	topaz
‖⌈	725	2298	305	topaz
⌊	471	6010	266	avocado, vy. lt.
L⌈	727	2289	293	topaz, vy. lt.
⌊	472	6253	264	avocado, ul. lt.
ε⌈	783	5307	307	gold
⌊	782	5308	308	topaz, med.
∧	783	5307	307	gold
♭	725	2298	305	topaz
⫽	726	2295	295	topaz, lt.
⌐	727	2289	293	topaz, vy. lt.
M⌈	986	6021	246	forest, vy. dk.
⌊	895	6021	246	green, dk.
G	904	6258	258	parrot green, vy. dk.
<	988	6258	243	forest, med.

COLONIAL FRUIT STACK

Symbol		DMC	Anchor	Color
U		988	6258	243	forest, med.
		472	6253	264	avocado, ul. lt.
·.		472	6253	264	avocado, ul. lt.
e		470	6010	267	avocado, lt.
		783	5307	307	gold
Z		720	2322	326	spice, dk.
		782	5308	308	topaz, med.
4		971	2099	314	pumpkin
		783	5307	307	gold
∧		741	2314	314	tangerine, med.
		783	5307	307	gold
C		742	2303	303	tangerine, lt.
		725	2298	305	topaz
6		320	6017	215	pistachio, med.
		471	6010	266	avocado, vy. lt.
X		368	6016	214	pistachio, lt.
		772	6250	253	pine green, lt.
/		772	6250	253	pine green, lt.

Symbol		DMC	Anchor	Color
¬		471	6010	266	avocado, vy. lt.
		470	6010	267	avocado, lt.
a		730	—	924	olive, vy. dk.
		934	6270	862	avocado black
N		732	—	281	olive
		434	5000	370	brown, lt.
'		733	—	280	olive, med.
		435	5371	363	brown, vy. lt.

Fabric: 28-count tea-dyed Irish linen from Charles Craft, Inc.
Stitch count: 159H x 130W
Design size:
25-count 12¾" x 10½"
28-count 11⅜" x 9¼"
30-count 10⅝" x 8⅝"
32-count 10" x 8⅛"

Instructions: Cross stitch over two threads, using two strands of floss. Backstitch using one strand of floss unless otherwise indicated. When two floss colors are bracketed together, use one strand of each.

Backstitch instructions:
433 5471 944 apple stems (two strands)
471 6010 266 veins on magnolia leaves
782 5308 308 remainder of magnolia leaves
3371 5478 382 remainder of backstitching

Designed by Cathy Livingston

Shaded portion indicates overlap from previous page.

(Continued on the next page)

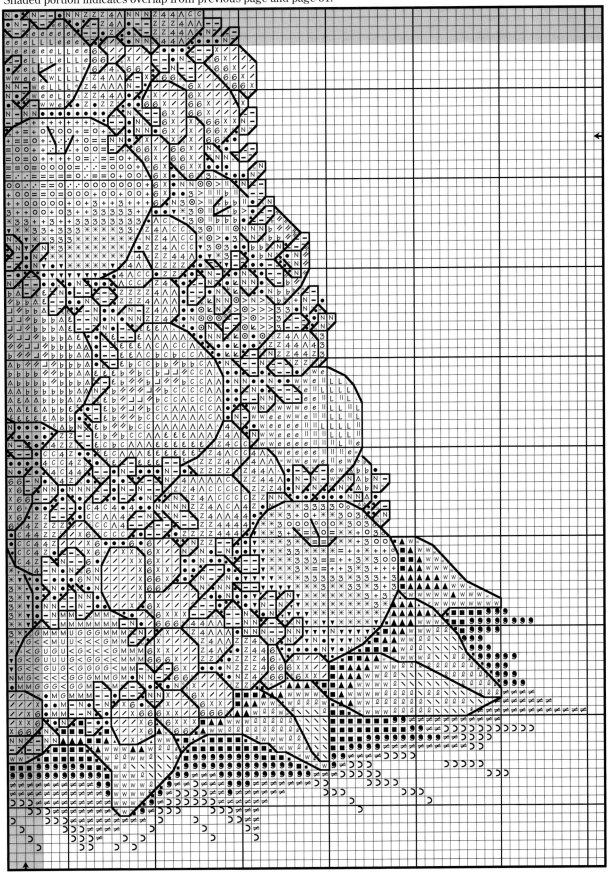

Friends

Chart begins on page 36.

Lily Maiden

Chart begins on page 38.

FRIENDS—TOP

36

Shaded portion indicates overlap from previous page.

FRIENDS

	DMC	Coats	Anchor®	
•	white	1001	01	white
∴	776	3281	25	pink, med.
T	3326	3126	36	rose, lt.
o	899	3282	38	rose, med.
◖	335	3283	38	rose
✕	309	3284	42	rose, dp.
■	326	3401	59	rose, vy. dp.
∙∙	818	3281	23	baby pink
╱	369	6015	260	pistachio, vy. lt.
Z	368	6016	214	pistachio, lt.
X	320	6017	215	pistachio, med.
C	367	6018	210	pistachio, dk.
✳	319	6246	246	pistachio, vy. dk.
♥	890	6021	212	pistachio, ul. dk.
‖	3348	6266	264	green, lt.
6	3347	6266	267	yellow-green, lt.
⍺	3346	6258	268	hunter
W	3345	6258	269	hunter, dk.
4	798	7022	131	delft, dk.
ε	552	4092	101	violet, dk.
λ	744	2293	301	yellow, pl.
2	794	—	175	cornflower, lt.
7	793	—	176	cornflower, med.
⊞	792	7150	177	cornflower, dk.
8	211	4303	342	lavender, lt.
e	210	4304	110	lavender, med.
ℓ	209	4302	110	lavender, dk.
P	742	2303	303	tangerine, lt.
↗	613	—	956	coffee brown, lt.
<	612	—	832	drab brown, med.
M	611	5898	898	drab brown, dk.
⊗	610	5889	889	drab brown, vy. dk.
bs	742	2303	303	tangerine, lt.

Fabric: 32-count ivory Jobelan from Wichelt Imports, Inc.

Stitch count: 148H x 114W

Design size:
25-count 11⅞" x 9⅛"
28-count 10⅝" x 8⅛"
30-count 9⅞" x 7⅝"
32-count 9¼" x 7⅛"

Instructions: Cross stitch over two threads, using two strands of floss. Backstitch using one strand of floss unless indicated otherwise. Make French knot where symbol ⊙ appears at tips of stamens on tiger lilies, using two strands 742/2303/303 and wrapping floss around needle once. See stitch illustration on page 40.

Backstitch (bs) instructions:
319 6246 246 all vines, stems, and leaves **except** ferns
3346 6258 268 ferns
890 6021 212 tendrils around large *M*, lettering (two strands)
792 7150 177 larger blue flowers
611 5898 898 stamens on tiger lilies
776 3281 25 remainder of tiger lilies
335 3283 38 pink buds at bottom of design

Designed by Angela Pullen

LILY MAIDEN—TOP

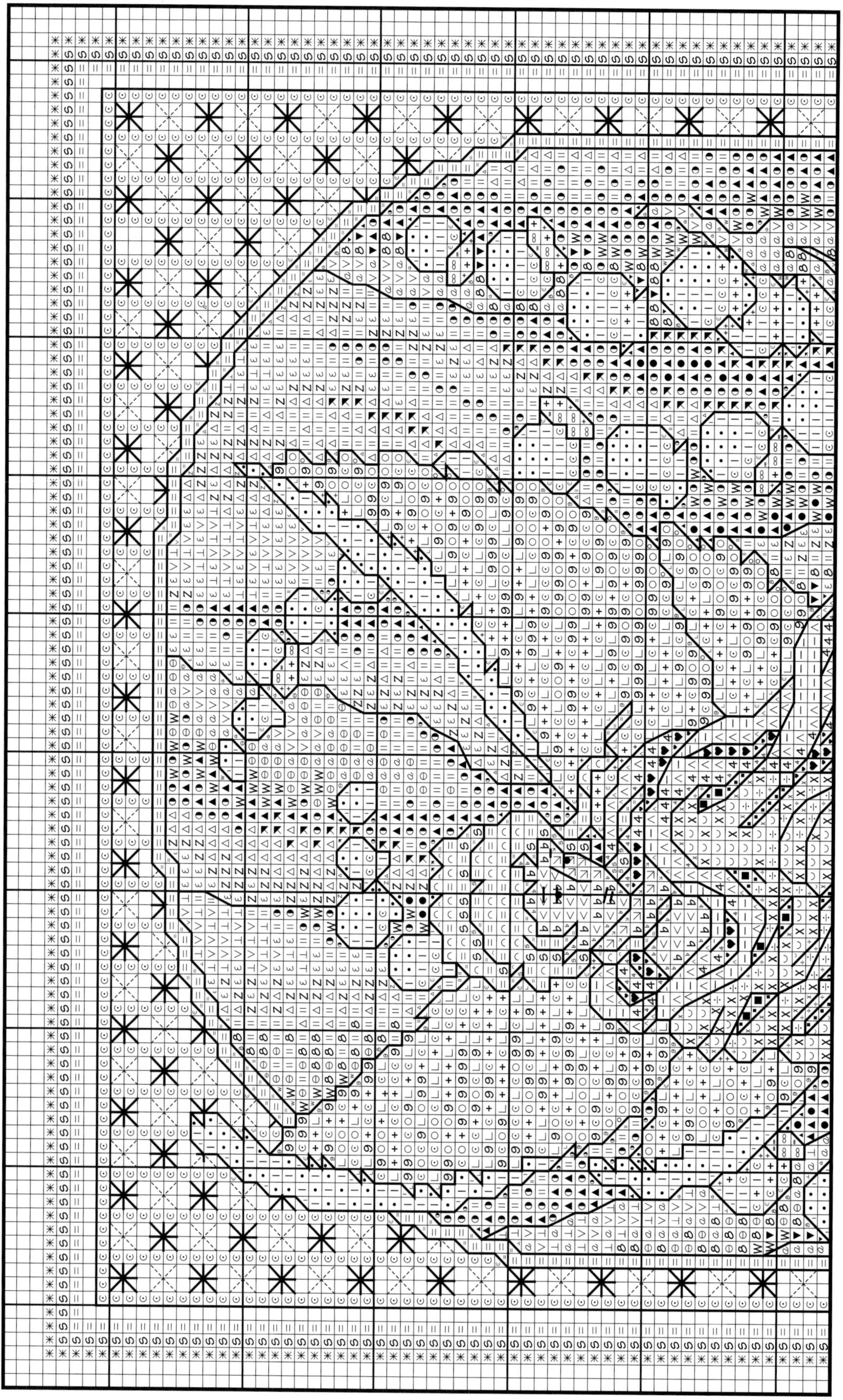

Shaded portion indicates overlap from previous page.

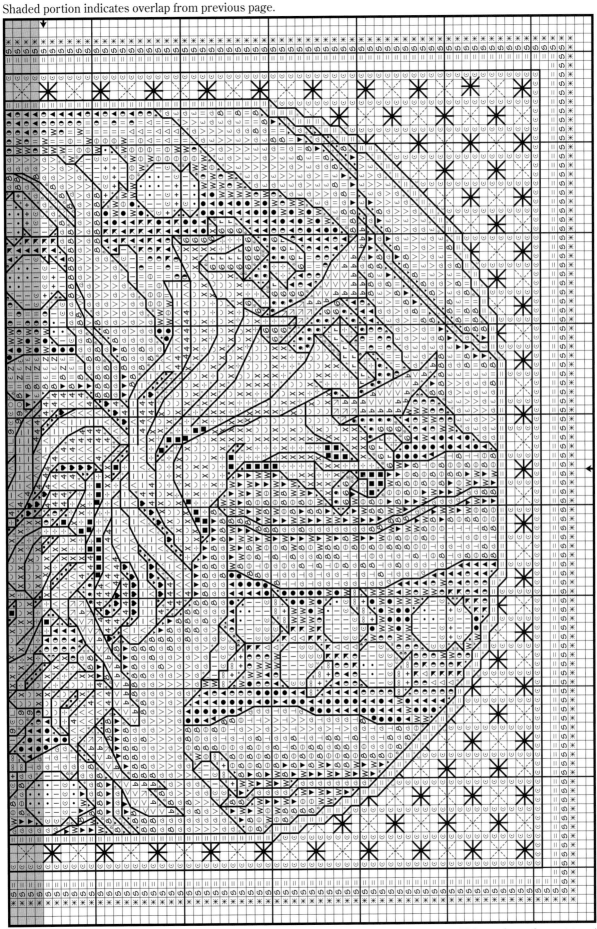

(Color code on the next page)

LILY MAIDEN

DMC Coats Anchor®

	DMC	Coats	Anchor®	
•	500	6880	879	blue-green, vy. dk.
W	501	6878	878	blue-green, dk.
⊖	502	6876	877	blue-green
⊥	503	6879	876	blue-green, med.
↘	3011	6845	845	khaki, dk.
△	3012	6843	844	khaki, med.
Z	3013	6842	842	khaki, lt.
▲	935	6270	861	avocado, dk.
◑	3362	6318	269	pine green, dk.
‖	3363	6317	262	pine green, med.
ε	3364	6010	843	pine green
S⌈	612	—	832	drab brown, med.
⌊	3046	2410	888	yellow-beige, lt.
=⌈	745	2350	300	yellow, lt. pl.
⌊	3047	2300	956	yellow-beige, lt.
∩	746	2275	275	off white
↘	950	2336	376	flesh, lt.
♭	3774	—	778	flesh, vy. lt.
<	3770	3334	—	flesh, vy. lt.
■	3726	3084	970	mauve, med. lt.
÷	316	3081	969	mauve, med.
X	778	3060	968	mauve, lt.
∪★	225	3239	892	pink, vy. lt.
♥⌈	340	7110	118	blue-violet, med.
⌊	3041	4222	871	antique violet, med.
4⌈	341	7005	117	blue-violet, lt.
⌊	3042	4221	869	antique-violet, lt.
∧⌈	3747	7004	120	blue-violet, vy. lt.
⌊	3743	—	869	antique-violet, vy. lt.
★⌈	3747	7004	120	blue-violet, vy. lt.
_⌊	white	1001	01	white
●⌈	3726	3084	970	mauve, med. lt.
⌊	451	8233	233	shell gray, dk.
6⌈	316	3081	969	mauve, med.
⌊	452	8232	232	shell gray, med.
r⌈	778	3060	968	mauve, lt.
⌊	453	8231	231	shell gray, lt.
▼⌈	520	6318	862	fern green, dk.
⌊	501	6878	878	blue-green, dk.
8⌈	522	6316	860	fern green
⌊	502	6876	877	blue-green
α⌈	523	6316	859	fern green, lt.
⌊	503	6879	876	blue-green, med.
∨⌈	524	6315	858	fern green, vy. lt.
⌊	504	6875	875	blue-green, lt.
∞	318	8511	399	steel gray, lt.
+⌈	318	8511	399	steel gray, lt.
⌊	415	8398	398	pearl gray
∈	415	8498	398	pearl gray
		762	8510	397	pearl gray, vy. lt.
•	white	1001	01	white
o⌈	762	8510	397	pearl gray, vy. lt.
⌊	746	2275	275	off white
9⌈	762	8510	397	pearl gray, vy. lt.
⌊	225	3239	892	pink, vy. lt.
⌊⌈	762	8510	397	pearl gray, vy. lt.
⌊	3747	7004	120	blue-violet, vy. lt.
✳	611	5898	898	drab brown, dk.
bs	414	8513	235	steel gray, dk.
	032BF Kreinik			pearl
	093BF Kreinik			star mauve

Fabric: 28-count antique white Brittney from Zweigart®

Stitch count: 120H x 96W

Design size:
25-count 9⅝" x 7⅝"
27-count 8⅞" x 7⅛"
28-count 8⅝" x 6⅞"
30-count 8" x 6½"

NOTE: Please read all instructions before beginning.

Instructions: Cross stitch over two threads, using two strands of floss. Backstitch using one strand of floss unless otherwise indicated. Make French knots where • appears for eyes, using two strands 611/5898/898 and wrapping floss around needle once. When ★ appears beside one floss color or two floss colors that are bracketed together, use one strand of floss colors listed and one strand 032BF Kreinik Metallics Blending Filament. When ◄ appears beside two floss colors that are bracketed together, stitch bottom half cross with blended colors and stitch top half cross using two strands 032BF Kreinik Metallics Blending Filament. When two colors are bracketed together, use one strand of each.

Backstitch (bs) instructions:

	DMC	Coats	Anchor	
	611	5898	898	facial features, hair, flesh, oval border
	3726	3084	970	mauve areas of clothing
	3041	4222	871	violet areas of clothing
	414	8513	235	wings, blooms
	520	6318	862	leaves
⌈	340	7110	118	inner border (one
⌊	3041	4222	871	strand of each)

Border instructions:
When cross stitching is complete, make Smyrna crosses where ✳ appears. Make first two stitches, which form a large X, using one strand each 522/6316/860 and 502/6876/877. Make third and fourth stitches, which form a large +, using one strand each 524/6315/858 and 504/6875/875. Straight stitch where - - - appears, using one strand 093BF Kreinik Metallics Blending Filament. Then stitch a small X at the intersection of the straight stitches, using one strand each 778/3060/968 and 3042/4221/869.

Designed by Teresa Wentzler

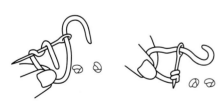

FRENCH KNOT

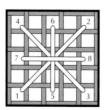

SMYRNA CROSS

Oriental Poppies

Chart begins on page 42.

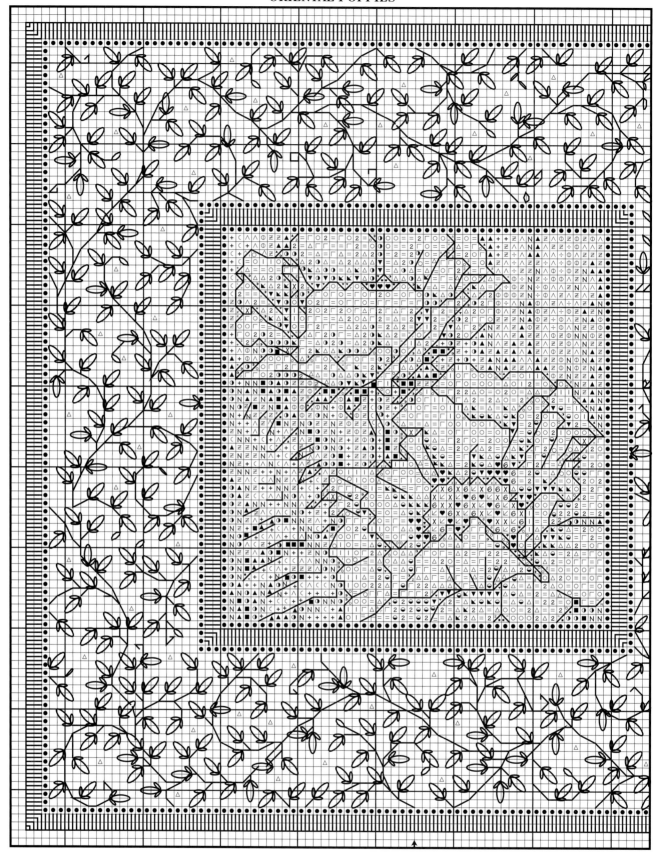

ORIENTAL POPPIES

DMC Coats Anchor®

	DMC	Coats	Anchor	Color
• [	500	6880	879	blue-green, vy. dk.
	935	6270	861	avocado, dk.
◑ [	501	6878	878	blue-green, dk.
	520	6318	862	fern green, dk.
N [	502	6876	877	blue-green
	522	6316	860	fern green
+ [	503	6879	876	blue-green, med.
	523	6316	859	fern green, lt.
C [	504	6875	875	blue-green, lt.
	524	6315	858	fern green, vy. lt.
▪ [	520	6318	862	fern green, dk.
	3051	6317	846	green-gray, dk.
▲ [	522	6316	860	fern green
	3052	6316	860	green-gray, med.
z [	523	6316	859	fern green, vy. lt.
	3053	6315	860	green-gray
◤ [	221	3242	897	pink, dk.
	3777	—	—	terra cotta, vy. dk.
△ [	3721	—	—	pink, dk.
	347	3013	13	salmon, dk.
= [	3722	—	896	pink, med.
	3328	3071	10	salmon, med.
○ [	223	3241	895	pink, med.
	3712	—	—	salmon, med.
I [	224	3240	894	pink, lt.
	760	3069	894	salmon
▼ [	221	3242	897	pink, dk.
	315	3082	972	mauve, dk.
◕ [	3721	—	—	pink, dk.
	3726	3084	970	mauve, med. lt.
2 [	3722	—	896	pink, med.
	316	3081	969	mauve, med.
┌ [	223	3241	895	pink, med.
	3727	—	969	mauve, lt.
♥	938	5477	381	coffee, ul. dk.
6 [	838	5381	380	beige-brown, vy. dk.
	3740	—	872	antique violet, dk.
⊾ [	839	5360	360	beige-brown, dk.
	3041	4222	871	antique violet, med.
X [	839	5360	360	beige-brown, dk.
	3726	3084	970	mauve, med. lt.
⊕ [	3052	6316	860	green-gray, lt.
	3045	2412	886	yellow-beige, dk.
∴ [	3053	6315	860	green-gray
	422	5372	942	hazelnut, lt.
∧ [	524	6315	858	fern green, vy. lt.
	3053	6315	860	green-gray
bs	841	5578	378	beige-brown, lt.
ld	436	5943	362	tan
ss	840	5379	379	beige-brown, med.
ss	420	5374	374	hazelnut, dk.
ss	680	2876	907	old gold, dk.

Fabric: 28-count teal green Brittney from Zweigart®
Stitch count: 100H x 100W

Design size:
25-count 8" x 8"
28-count 7⅛" x 7⅛"
30-count 6⅝" x 6⅝"
32-count 6¼" x 6¼"

Instructions: Cross stitch over two threads, using two strands of floss. Back-stitch using one strand of floss. When two colors are bracketed together, use one strand of each. Make lazy-daisy stitches (ld) where ◠ appears, using **one strand each** 841/5578/378, 3045/2412/886, and 436/5943/362. Make satin stitches (ss) using **one strand each** 840/5379/379, 420/5374/374, and 680/2876/907. When satin stitch is completed, work chain stitch between cross stitch and satin stitch in borders, using one strand 221/3242/897.

Backstitch (bs) instructions:

841	5578	378	stems in border
839	5360	360	flower petals
938	5477	381	outer edge of design, center of right flower, brown areas of left flower
500	6880	879	remainder of back-stitching

Designed by Teresa Wentzler

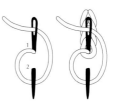

LAZY-DAISY STITCH

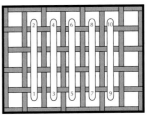

SATIN STITCH

CHAIN STITCH

HOPE CHEST COLLECTION

*T*he hope chest carries with it a history rich with tradition. A refined cousin of the medieval dowry, it has become, over the years, a visible sign of unspoken dreams. Though its popularity has waned during the last half-century, many young ladies still continue the tradition of filling a cedar chest with the treasures that will form the nucleus of a household when they marry. The "Hope Chest Collection," a special group of items to stitch and cherish, is our way of affirming this endearing tradition. Stitch the collection for yourself, your daughter, a niece, and dream of the future . . . .

Above—*Wreath of Spring Flowers,* page 52; Left (clockwise from top left)—*His & Her Afghan,* page 48; *Wedding Announcement Border,* page 46; and *Victorian Floral,* page 59.

Wedding Announcement Border

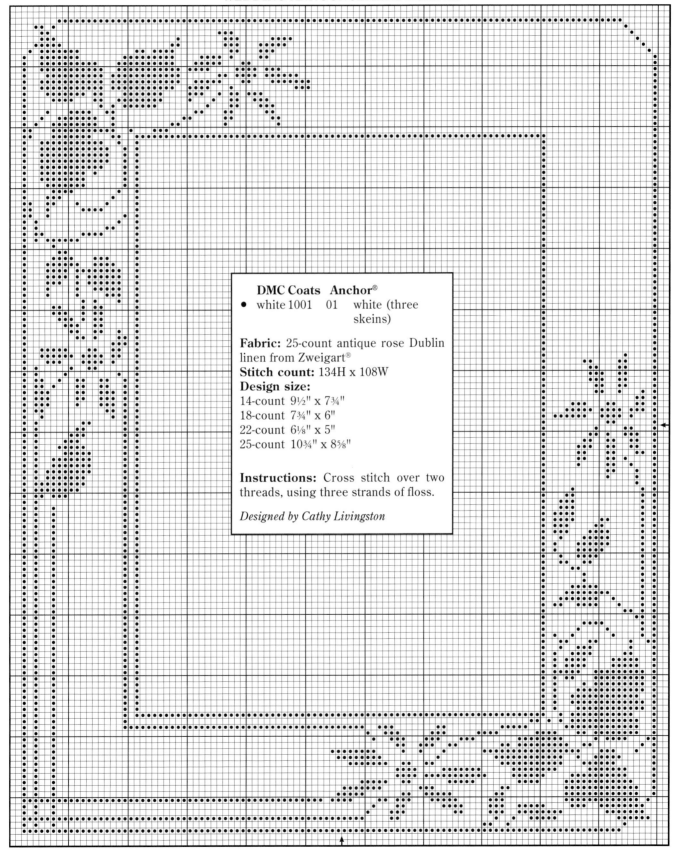

DMC Coats Anchor®
- white 1001   01   white (three skeins)

Fabric: 25-count antique rose Dublin linen from Zweigart®
Stitch count: 134H x 108W
Design size:
14-count 9½" x 7¾"
18-count 7¾" x 6"
22-count 6⅛" x 5"
25-count 10¾" x 8⅝"

Instructions: Cross stitch over two threads, using three strands of floss.

Designed by Cathy Livingston

His & Her Afghan

DMC
Coton Perlé #3 (Pearl Cotton)
white (24 skeins)

Fabric: 14-count antique white Lady Elizabeth afghan from Charles Craft, Inc.
Stitch count: 82H x 82W
NOTE: Completed afghan is approximately 45½" x 54½".
Design size:
11-count 7½" x 7½"
14-count 5⅞" x 5⅞"
18-count 4⅝" x 4⅝"
22-count 3¾" x 3¾"

Instructions: Stitch using one strand coton perlé, cut at least 25" long. To stitch each motif, begin in center and follow graph, stitching over number of threads indicated and being careful not to pull too tightly. Alternate motifs in checkerboard style.

Special instructions:
Graph A:
Center: Stitch a block of four mosaic stitches, working each mosaic stitch with seven stitches covering sixteen squares. Work mosaic stitches in alternate directions.
Row 1: Work twelve Algerian eye stitches bordering center mosaic block. Work each eyelet with eight stitches over two threads.
Skip two threads.
Row 2: Work single row of backstitching over two threads, placing ten stitches on each side of design.
Skip two threads.
Row 3: Work graduated satin stitch, stitching over four, three, two, three, and then four threads. Stitch twenty-five stitches per row on each side of design. To complete pattern, refer to chart for stitch placement, allowing stitches over four threads to meet.
Row 3 corners: To work each corner, stitch four long stitches over five threads to form a diamond, placing inside points in same hole where two

(Continued on the next page)

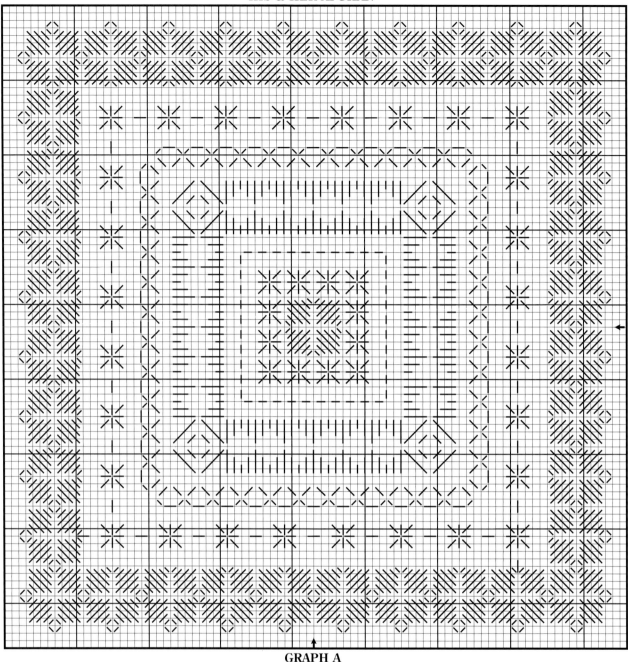

GRAPH A

longest stitches of satin stitches meet. Work small diamond in center of large diamond.

Skip one thread.

Row 4: Work series of backstitches to create pattern covering four threads (three squares). Repeat pattern eleven times on each side of square.

Skip two threads.

Row 5: For each side of square, work Algerian eye stitches, alternating with straight stitches. Each side consists of eight Algerian eye stitches (including corners) and seven straight stitches.

NOTE: Remember to include Algerian eyes in corners when counting the stitches on each side.

Skip two threads.

Row 6: Work mosaic stitch around block, alternating direction of stitches and completing eighteen stitches on each side.

Row 7: Work mosaic stitch next to Row 6, alternating direction of stitches. **NOTE:** Add two extra stitches over two threads (one square) to alternate junctions of completed stitches to form a "picot" around outside of row.

Graph B:

Center: Count three threads from center to begin each petal.

Petal borders: Work each border using Smyrna or double cross stitches. Each square on graph (covering four

squares) represents one completed double cross. Cross all stitches in the same direction.

Petal insides: Work inside of each petal using Algerian eye or fern stitch variation, working each stitch over three threads. Add additional straight stitches to fill in each petal as needed.

Finishing: Count out ten threads from woven border and work Nun's stitch over three threads in each direction along all four sides. Trim edges to 2½" away from edge of Nun's stitch and pull threads to edge of Nun's stitch to fringe.

Designed by Linda Gordanier Jary

50

GRAPH B

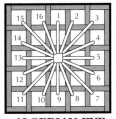

ALGERIAN EYE

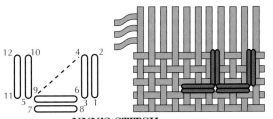

NUN'S STITCH

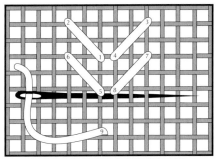

FERN STITCH VARIATION

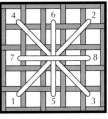

SMYRNA CROSS

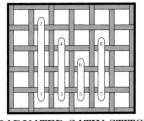

GRADUATED SATIN STITCH

Floral Fantasies

VICTORIAN FAN

DMC Coats Anchor®

	DMC	Coats	Anchor®	
+	471	6266	266	avocado green, vy. lt.
ℓ	470	6010	267	avocado green, lt.
•	937	6268	268	avocado green, med.
C	3328	3071	10	salmon, med.
X	347	3013	13	salmon, dk.
ε	211	4303	342	lavender, lt.
✒	209	4302	110	lavender, dk.
/	677	5372	886	old gold, vy. lt.
V	676	—	887	old gold, lt.
Z	729	2875	874	old gold, med.
o	white	1001	01	white
⁄⁄	746	2275	275	off white
■	347	3013	13	salmon, dk.

Fabric: 14-count ivory damask Victorian envelope pillow from The Janlynn® Corporation

Stitch count: 54H x 64W

Design size:
11-count 5" x 6"
14-count 4" x 4¾"
18-count 3" x 3¾"
22-count 2⅜" x 3"

Instructions: Cross stitch using two strands of floss. Backstitch using one strand of floss. Make French knots using two strands 347/3013/13, wrapping floss around needle twice. Make French knots in center of small purple flowers using same color as flowers. Purchase ½ yd. 1/16"-wide lavender satin ribbon for bow.

Backstitch instructions:
Backstitch in order listed.

470	6010	267	all stems
676	—	887	cream flower
211	4303	342	dark purple petals
209	4302	110	light purple petals
347	3013	13	red flower
white	1001	01	white flowers
676	—	887	fan outline

Designed by Keith Lawler

VICTORIAN FAN

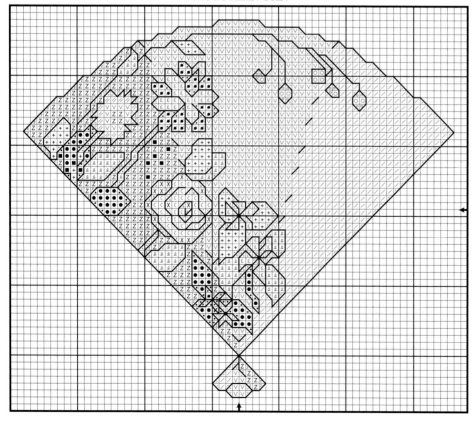

WREATH OF SPRING FLOWERS

DMC Coats Anchor®

W	349	2335	13	coral, dk.
6	350	3111	11	coral, med.
>	352	3008	9	coral, lt.
Z	3705	3012	35	melon, dk.
∧	3706	3127	33	melon, med.
O	3708	3127	31	melon, lt.
·	white	1001	01	white
II	415	8393	398	pearl gray
⊙	721	2324	324	orange spice, med.
+	742	2303	303	tangerine, lt.
V	743	2302	302	yellow, med.
/	744	2293	301	yellow, pl.
∵	727	2289	293	topaz, vy. lt.
L	725	2298	305	topaz
*	783	5307	307	Christmas gold
M	333	—	119	blue violet, dk.
4	340	7110	118	blue violet, med.
-	341	7005	117	blue violet, lt.
K	792	7150	177	cornflower blue, dk.
=	793	—	176	cornflower blue, med.
\	794	—	175	cornflower blue, lt.
●	3345	6258	269	hunter green, dk.
3	3346	6258	268	hunter green
X	3347	6266	267	yellow-green, med.
I	3348	6266	264	yellow-green, lt.
bs	414	8513	235	steel gray, dk.
bs	782	5308	308	topaz, med.
bs	741	2314	314	tangerine, med.

Fabric: 14-count ivory damask Victorian pillow from The Janlynn® Corporation
Stitch count: 91H x 96W
Design size:

11-count 8¼" x 8¾"
14-count 6½" x 6¾"
18-count 5" x 5¼"
22-count 4¼" x 4½"

Instructions: Cross stitch using two strands of floss. Backstitch using one strand of floss.

Backstitch (bs) instructions:

741	2314	314	daffodils
414	8513	235	white narcissus
3705	3012	35	tulips
349	2335	13	coral roses
782	5308	308	yellow roses
792	7150	177	iris
333	—	119	grape hyacinths
3345	6258	269	leaves

Designed by Cathy Livingston

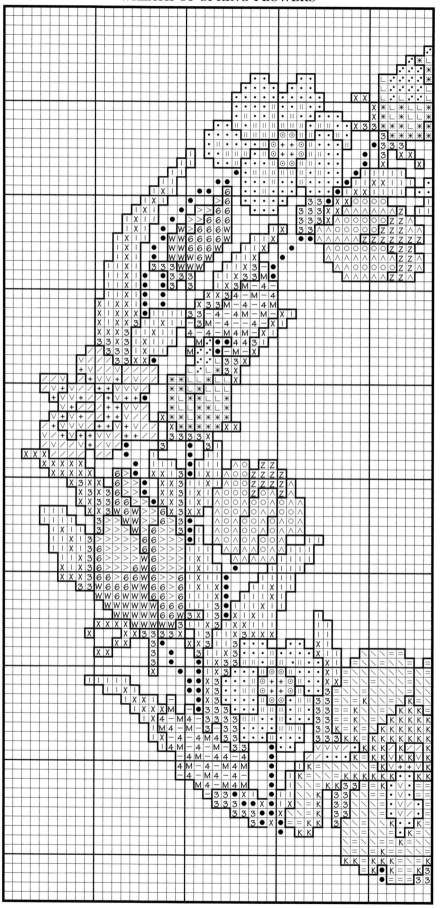

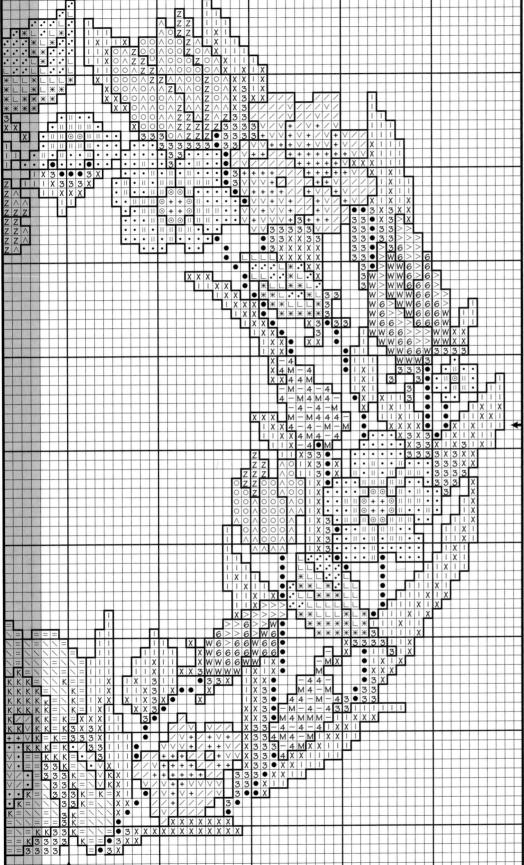

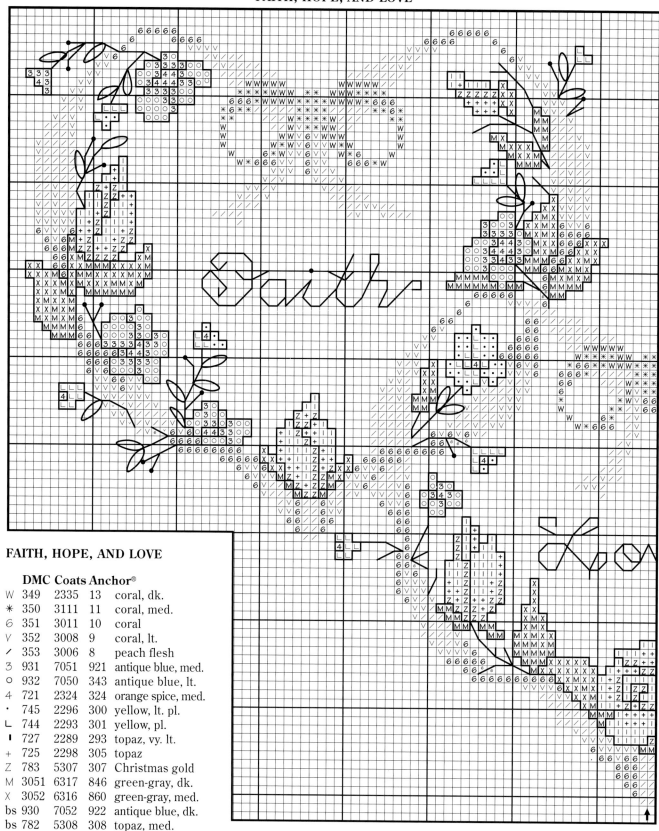

FAITH, HOPE, AND LOVE

DMC Coats Anchor®

	DMC	Coats	Anchor®	
W	349	2335	13	coral, dk.
✳	350	3111	11	coral, med.
6	351	3011	10	coral
V	352	3008	9	coral, lt.
╱	353	3006	8	peach flesh
3	931	7051	921	antique blue, med.
O	932	7050	343	antique blue, lt.
4	721	2324	324	orange spice, med.
•	745	2296	300	yellow, lt. pl.
L	744	2293	301	yellow, pl.
I	727	2289	293	topaz, vy. lt.
+	725	2298	305	topaz
Z	783	5307	307	Christmas gold
M	3051	6317	846	green-gray, dk.
X	3052	6316	860	green-gray, med.
bs	930	7052	922	antique blue, dk.
bs	782	5308	308	topaz, med.
bs	935	6270	861	avocado green, dk.
bs	743	2302	302	yellow, med.

Fabric: 14-count ivory damask Victorian pillow from The Janlynn® Corporation
Stitch count: 89H x 148W

Shaded portion indicates overlap from previous page.

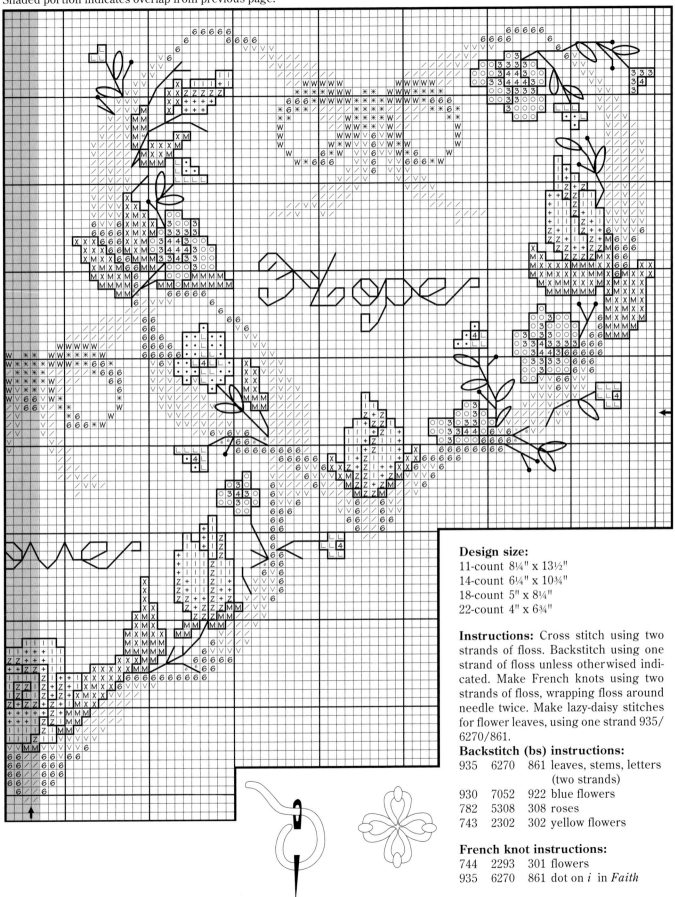

Design size:
11-count 8¼" x 13½"
14-count 6¼" x 10¾"
18-count 5" x 8¼"
22-count 4" x 6¾"

Instructions: Cross stitch using two strands of floss. Backstitch using one strand of floss unless otherwised indicated. Make French knots using two strands of floss, wrapping floss around needle twice. Make lazy-daisy stitches for flower leaves, using one strand 935/6270/861.

Backstitch (bs) instructions:

935	6270	861 leaves, stems, letters (two strands)
930	7052	922 blue flowers
782	5308	308 roses
743	2302	302 yellow flowers

French knot instructions:

744	2293	301 flowers
935	6270	861 dot on *i* in *Faith*

LAZY-DAISY STITCH

Designed by Cathy Livingston

Wedding Treasures

Charts begin on page 60.

Victorian Floral

Chart begins on page 64.

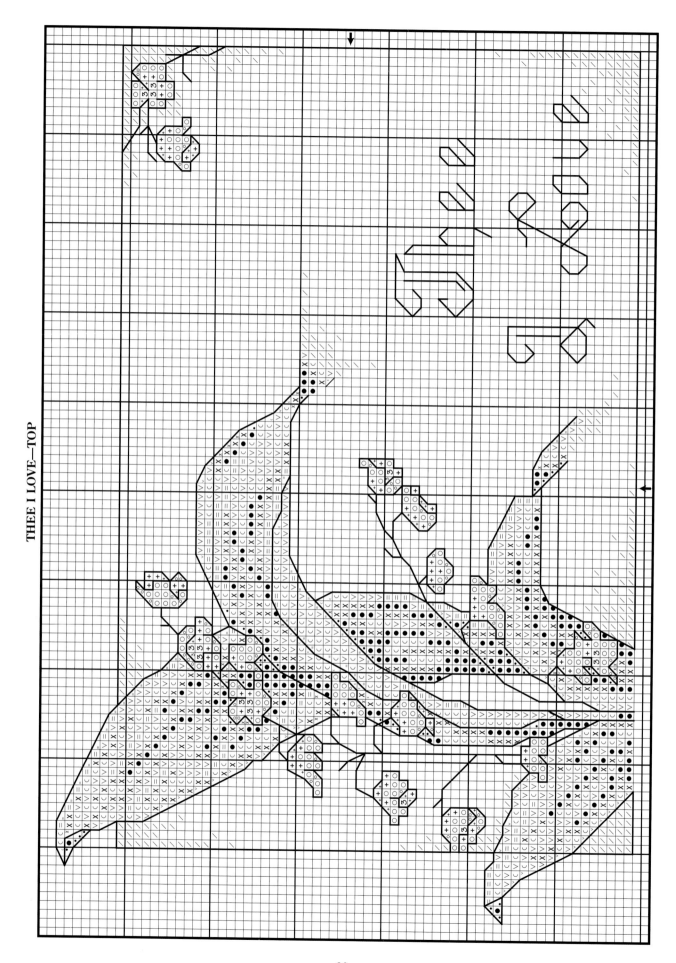

THEE I LOVE

DMC Coats Anchor®

- ● 319 6246 218 pistachio green, vy. dk.
- X 367 6018 217 pistachio green, dk.
- C 320 6017 215 pistachio green, med.
- V 368 6016 214 pistachio green, lt.
- = 369 6015 259 pistachio green, vy. lt.
- o white 1001 01 white
- + 415 8398 398 pearl gray
- з 745 2296 300 yellow, lt. pl.
- ∕ 368 6016 214 pistachio green, lt. **(half cross)**
- bs 890 6021 — pistachio green, ul. dk.
- bs 317 8512 400 pewter gray

Fabric: 25-count moss green Lugana from Zweigart®
Stitch count: 67H x 98W
Design size:
11-count 6" x 9"
14-count 4¾" x 7"
18-count 3¾" x 5½"
22-count 3" x 4½"
25-count 2⅝" x 3⅞"

Instructions: Cross stitch over two threads, using two strands of floss. Backstitch using one strand of floss unless otherwise indicated.
Backstitch (bs) instructions:
317 8512 400 flowers
319 6246 218 tip of bottom-left leaf, bottom edge of lower-right leaf, lower left side and tip of large background leaf
320 6017 215 bottom-left leaf **except** for tip, upper-left side to tip of large background leaf, bottom-right edge and left side of large center leaf to tip
368 6016 214 top of lower-right leaf, right side of large background leaf
369 6015 259 center line in large center leaf
890 6021 — flower stems, letters, border (two strands)

Designed by Cathy Livingston

BRIDE'S BIBLE COVER

Bride's
DMC Coats Anchor®

- ∕ 778 3060 — antique mauve, lt.
- X 316 3081 — antique mauve, med.
- ⌐ 3053 6315 — green-gray
- 8 3052 6316 — green-gray, med.
- I 524 6315 858 fern green, vy. lt.
- з 523 6316 859 fern green, lt.
- o 504 6875 213 blue green, lt.
- ● 503 6879 875 blue green, med.
- 6 928 7225 848 gray-green, lt.
- ★ 927 6006 849 gray-green, med.
- ∙∙ 3047 2300 — yellow-beige, lt.
- V 3046 2410 887 yellow-beige, med.
- ∙ ecru 1002 387 ecru
- S 3033 5388 391 mocha brown, vy. lt.
- + 3032 5393 903 mocha brown, med.
- ■ 451 8233 233 shell gray, dk.
- bs 315 8512 — antique mauve, dk.
- bs 502 6876 877 blue green
- bs 926 6007 850 gray-green, dk.

NOTE: Optional *Commemorative* design is given for center of *Bride's Bible Cover.*

Commemorative
DMC Coats Anchor®

- ∕ 603 3001 62 cranberry
- X 601 3128 57 cranberry, dk.
- ⌐ 581 6256 — moss green
- 8 580 6267 — moss green, dk.
- I 3347 6266 266 yellow-green, med.
- з 3345 6258 — hunter green, dk.
- o 503 6879 875 blue green, med.
- ● 501 6878 878 blue green, dk.
- 6 794 — 175 cornflower blue, lt.
- ★ 798 7022 131 delft, med.
- ∙∙ 677 — 886 old gold, vy. lt.
- V 676 2874 891 old gold, lt.
- ∙ white 1001 01 white
- S 762 8510 397 pearl gray, vy. lt.
- – 840 5379 — beige brown, med.
- + 839 5360 — beige brown, dk.
- 2 3064 3883 883 sportsman flesh, med.
- 4 632 5936 936 brown, dk.
- ■ 3371 5478 382 black-brown
- bs 815 3000 44 garnet, med.
- bs 500 6880 879 blue green, vy. dk.
- bs 824 7182 164 blue, vy. dk.

Fabric: 27-count white Super Linen from Charles Craft, Inc.
Stitch count: 140H x 112W
Design size:
11-count 12¾" x 10¼"
14-count 10" x 8"
18-count 8" x 6¼"
22-count 6½" x 5¼"
27-count 5⅛" x 4⅛"

Instructions: Cross stitch over two threads, using two strands of floss. Backstitch using two strands of floss. See center of main chart. Personalize and date, if desired, centering lettering and using alphabet and numerals provided.
Backstitch (bs) instructions:
Bride's
926 6007 850 ribbon
502 6876 877 leaves, leaf veins, rose stems
315 8512 — roses
3032 5393 903 ivy vine, stems
451 8233 233 remainder of backstitching
Commemorative
500 6880 879 leaves, leaf veins, rose stems
815 3000 44 roses
839 5360 — ivy vine, stems
824 7182 164 ribbon, remainder of backstitching

Finishing instructions: Measure Bible or book for fabric needed, allowing enough fabric for seams. Purchase trim and satin for edging and lining. Work design on right-hand end of fabric. Sew satin and trim to right side of fabric, as shown in illustration. Place lining atop right side of fabric and sew together. Trim seams and turn. Press. Whipstitch lace to edge of cover.

Designed by Dot Young

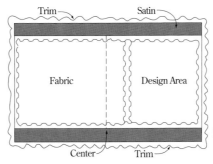

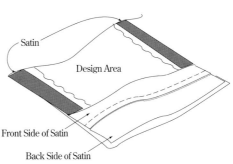

(Chart is on the next page.)

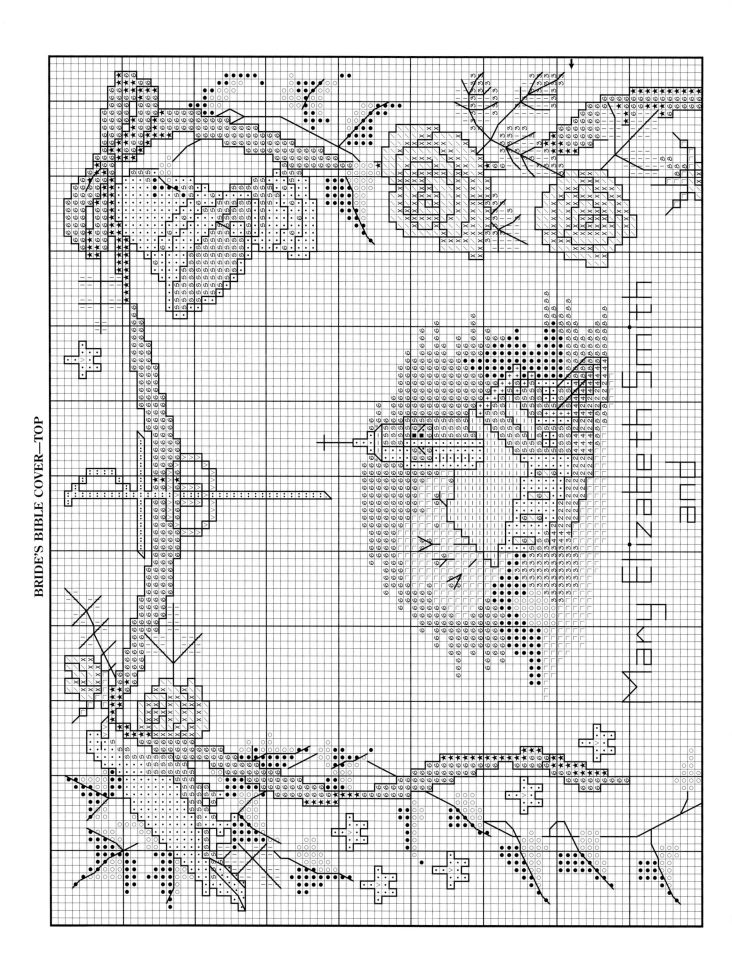

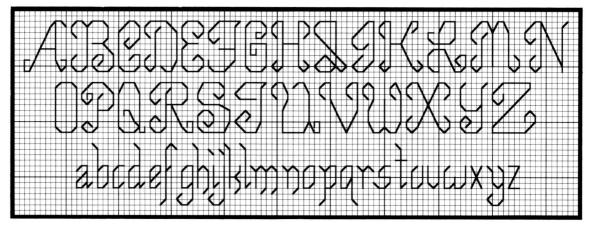

Shaded portion indicates overlap from previous page.

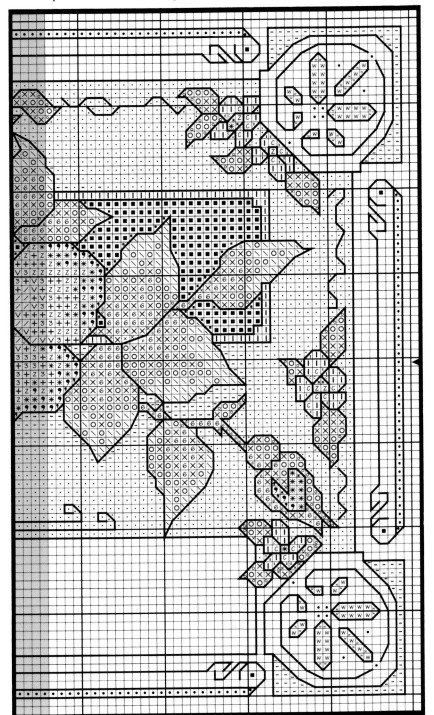

VICTORIAN FLORAL

DMC Coats Anchor®

	DMC	Coats	Anchor®	
C ⌈	746	2275	275	off white
⌊	928	7225	274	gray-green, lt.
I	746	2275	275	off white
╱	677	—	886	old gold, vy. lt.
V ⌈	676	2305	887	old gold, lt.
⌊	727	2289	293	topaz, vy. lt.
3 ⌈	676	2305	887	old gold, lt.
⌊	722	2323	323	spice, lt.
+ ⌈	722	2323	323	spice, lt.
⌊	729	2875	874	old gold, med.
Z	721	2324	324	spice, med.
* ⌈	680	2876	907	old gold, dk.
⌊	721	2324	324	spice, med.
❷	720	2322	326	spice, dk.
W	729	2875	874	old gold, med.
●	680	2876	907	old gold, dk.
6	936	6269	269	avocado, vy. dk.
X	469	6261	268	avocado
O	470	6010	267	avocado, lt.
╲	471	6010	266	avocado, vy. lt.
-	926	6007	850	gray-green, dk.
·	927	6006	848	gray-green, med.
■	420	5374	374	hazelnut, dk.
bs	934	6270	862	avocado-black

Fabric: 25-count cream Lugana® from Zweigart®
Stitch count: 79H x118W
Design size:
14-count 5⅝" x 8½"
18-count 4⅜" x 6⅝"
25-count 6⅜" x 9½"
27-count 5⅞" x 8¾"

Instructions: Cross stitch over two threads, using two strands of floss. Backstitch using one strand of floss. Make French knots using two strands of floss, wrapping floss around needle twice. When two floss colors are bracketed together, use one strand of each.
NOTE: Center names in space provided, using alphabet given.

Backstitch (bs) instructions:
934 6270 862 flowers, leaves
420 5374 374 remainder of back-
                         stitching

French knot instructions:
469 6261 268 make cluster of knots
                         where symbol 6 ap-
                         pears in center of
                         each large flower

Designed by Cathy Livingston

SAMPLERS

Samplers possess one of the strongest links to our needleworking heritage of any type of needlework in existence. Created during times past by young girls learning household skills, the samplers of days gone by were testaments to young ladies' preparation for marriage and adult life. The sampler, which most often contained alphabets, numerals, and decorative motifs, was comprised of a sampling of stitches. It was frequently used as an educational tool to teach ABCs, numerals, and, more importantly, a mastery of various stitches and techniques. The sampler has found its way through the centuries from the utilitarian workboxes of long ago to prized spots of display in households throughout America and the world.

Above—*House Sampler,* page 68; Left (clockwise from top left)—*Crown Sampler,* page 69; *Hands to Work Sampler,* page 81; *Demarest Adaptation Sampler,* page 78; and *Neighbor's Blessings Sampler,* page 86.

House Sampler

Chart begins on page 70.

Crown Sampler

Chart begins on page 72.

HOUSE SAMPLER

DMC Coats Anchor®

▲	3051	6317	846	green-gray, dk.
╱	3052	6316	—	green-gray, med.
+	3053	6315	—	green-gray
∪	3328	3071	—	salmon, med.
X	950	2336	—	sportsman flesh, lt.
∩	926	6007	850	gray-green, dk.
T	927	6006	849	gray-green, med.
–	928	7225	848	gray-green, lt.
╲	3041	4222	871	antique violet, med.
⊃	3042	4221	870	antique violet, lt.
Y	647	8900	858	beaver gray, med.
■	3045	2412	888	yellow beige, dk.
⊥	739	5369	885	tan, ul. lt.
C	745	2296	300	yellow, lt. pl.
I	644	5831	899	beige-gray, med.
◥	3047	2300	—	yellow-beige, lt.

Fabric: 29-count cream linen from Anne Powell Ltd.
Stitch count: 176H x 158W
Design size:
25-count 14⅛" x 12¾"
27-count 13⅛" x 11¾"
29-count 12¼" x12¾"
30-count 11¾" x 10⅝"
32-count 11" x 9⅞"
35-count 10⅛" x 9⅛"

Instructions: Cross stitch over two threads, using two strands of floss. Work long-arm cross stitch for symbol ▲ in ground area under trees and house, using 3051/6317/846. Straight stitch bird's legs using 3045/2412/888. Work large alphabet in eyelet stitch.

Designed by Phyllis Hoffman

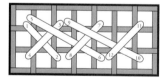

LONG-ARM CROSS STITCH

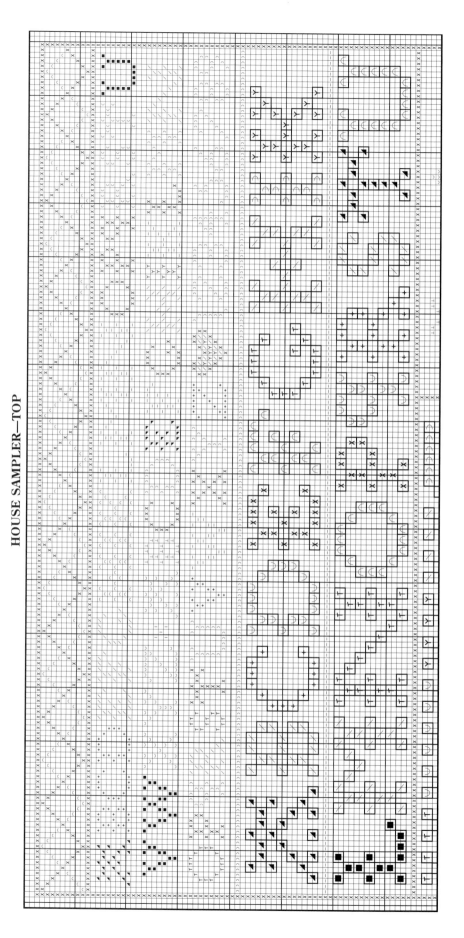

HOUSE SAMPLER—TOP

Shaded portion indicates overlap from previous page.

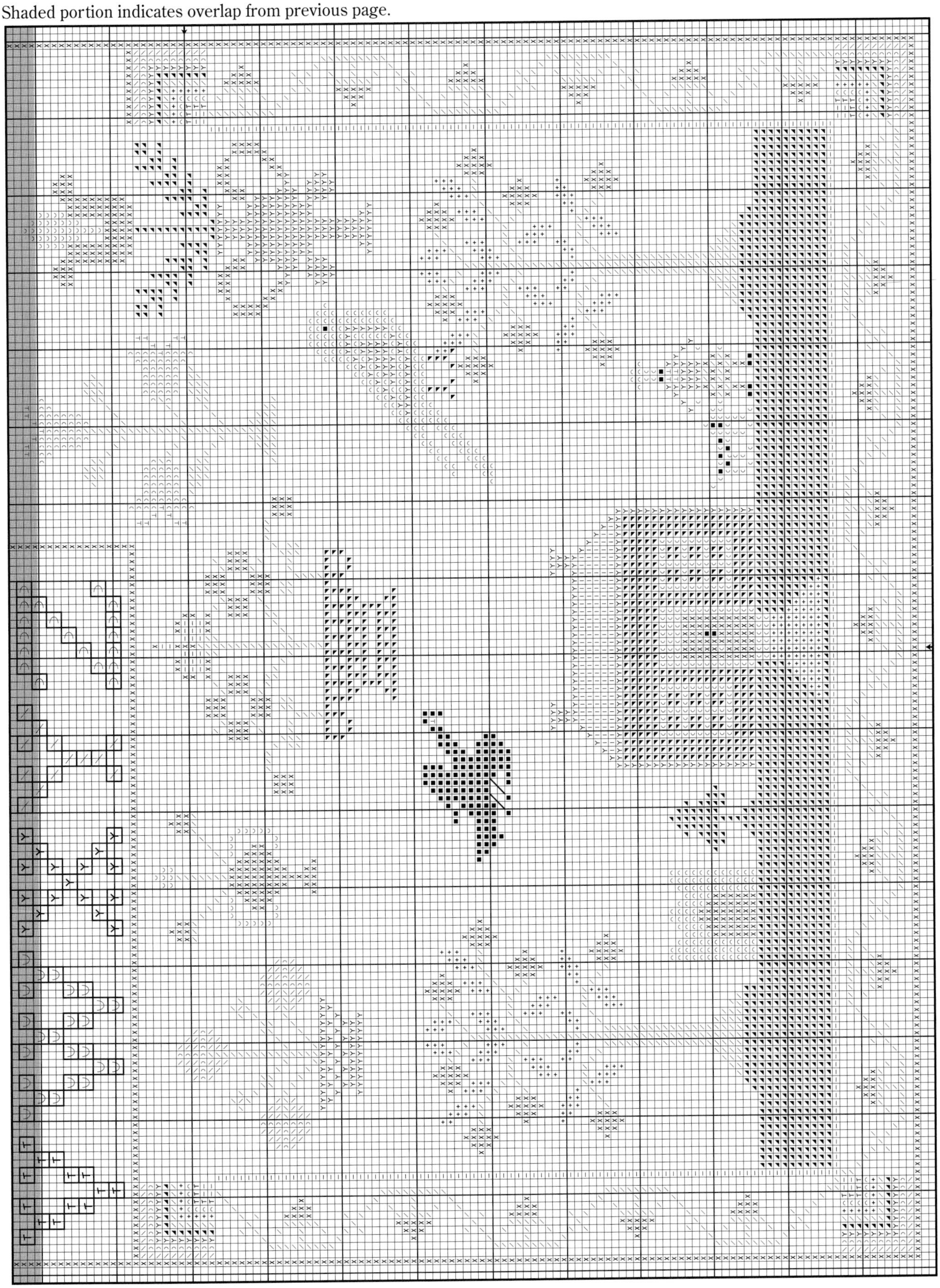

CROWN SAMPLER

DMC Coats Anchor®

■	501	6878	878	blue green, dk.
X	3328	3071	10	salmon, med.
◢	930	7052	922	antique blue, dk.
I	612	—	832	drab brown, med.
+	760	3069	894	salmon

Fabric: 30-count white linen from Wichelt Imports, Inc.

Stitch count: 158H x 132W

Design size:
11-count 14⅜" x 12"
14-count 11¼" x 9½"
18-count 8¾" x 7⅜"
22-count 7¼" x 6"
30-count 10½" x 8¾"

Instructions: Cross stitch over two threads, using two strands of floss. Work initials and date using sampler alphabet and numerals.

CROWN SAMPLER—TOP

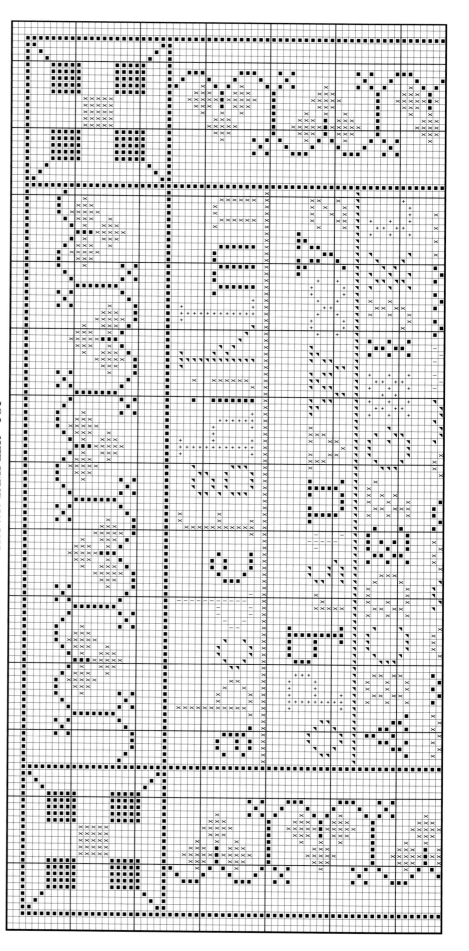

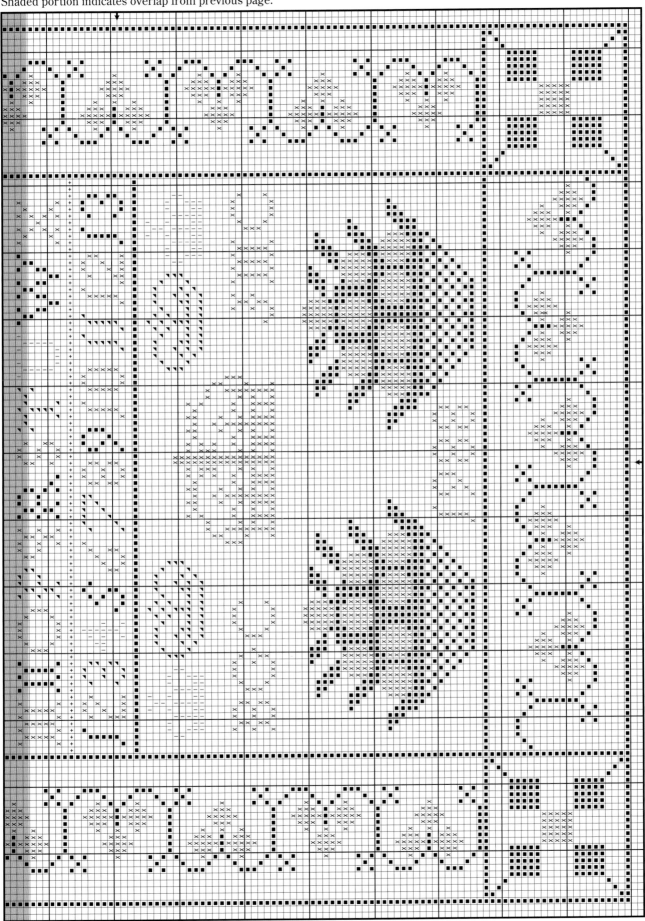

Psalm 100 Sampler

DMC	Coats	Anchor®	
●	935	6270	861 avocado, dk.
X	3051	6317	846 green-gray, dk.
L	3052	6316	860 green-gray, med.
6	221	3242	897 pink, dk.
o	223	3241	895 pink, med.
/	ecru	1002	387 ecru
3	420	5374	374 hazelnut, dk.
W	931	7051	921 antique blue, med.
C	932	7050	343 antique blue, lt.
=	676	2874	887 old gold, lt.
ss	3053	6315	860 green-gray

Fabric: 28-count tea-dyed linen from Charles Craft, Inc.
Stitch count: 139H x 91W

Design size:
25-count 11⅛" x 7¼"
28-count 10" x 6½"
30-count 9¼" x 6⅛"
32-count 8¾" x 5¾"

Instructions: Cross stitch over two threads, using two strands of floss, unless otherwise indicated.

Special instructions:
Row 1: Work four-sided stitch using two strands 932/7050/343.
Row 2: Work eyelet stitch using one strand 223/324/895.
Row 3: Work rice stitch over two threads, using two strands 676/2874/887.
Row 4: Work four-sided stitch using two strands 3052/6316/860.

Area 1: Cross stitch over one thread, using one strand of floss.
Area 2: Work satin stitch using two strands of floss. Work upper two rows using 3052/6316/860 and lower two rows using 3053/6315/860. Direction and individual placement of each satin stitch is shown on chart.
Area 3a: Cross stitch border over one thread, using one strand 3051/6317/846. Backstitch using one strand 3051/6317/846.
Area 3b: Backstitch using one strand 3051/6317/846.
Area 4: Work queen stitch using two strands of color indicated.

Designed by Cathy Livingston

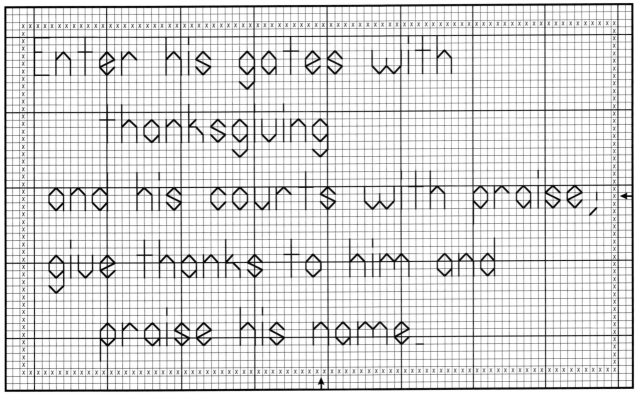

Area 3a

(Charts continued on the next page)

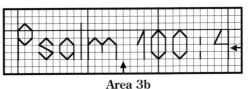

Area 3b

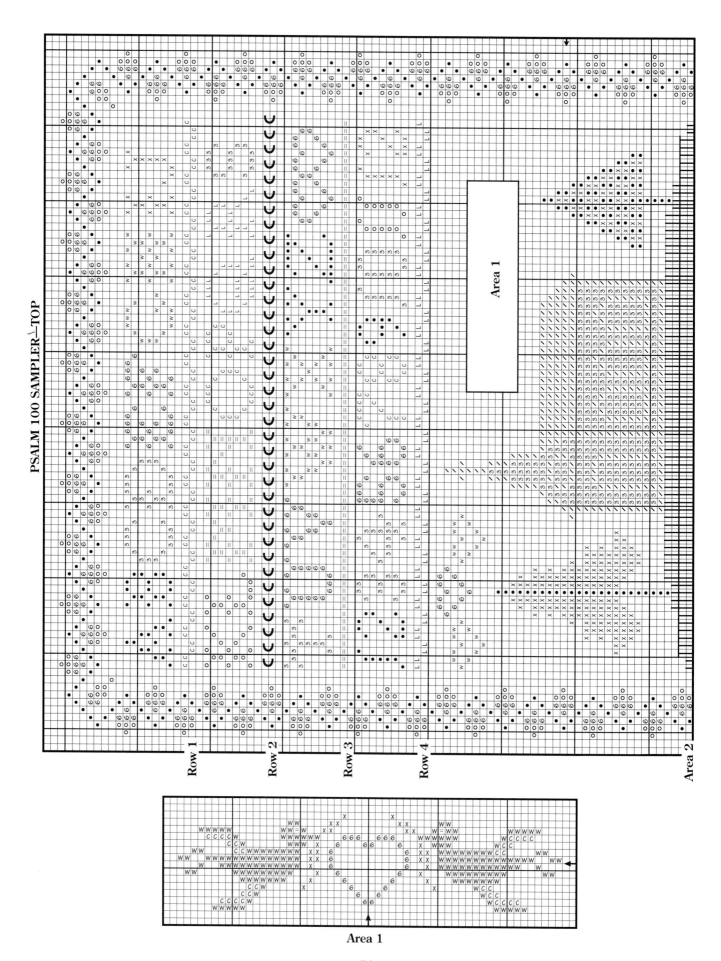

PSALM 100 SAMPLER—TOP

Area 1

Row 1
Row 2
Row 3
Row 4

Area 2

Area 1

Shaded portion indicates overlap from previous page.

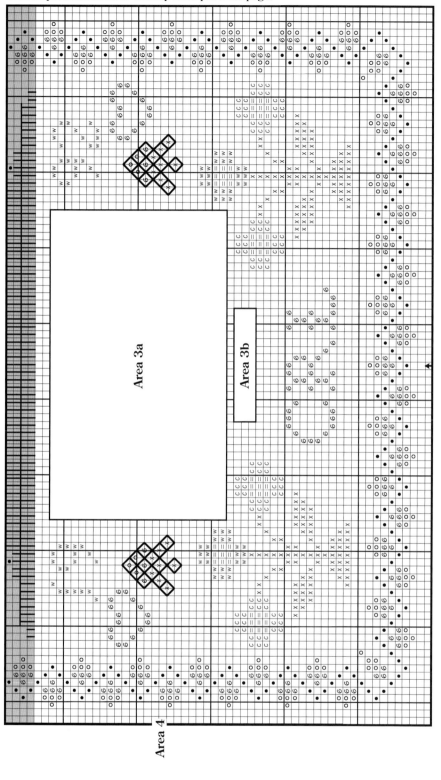

Area 3a

Area 3b

Area 4

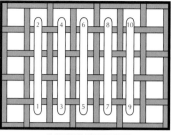

SATIN STITCH

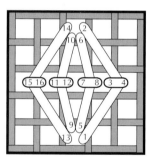

RICE STITCH

EYELET STITCH

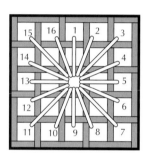

QUEEN STITCH

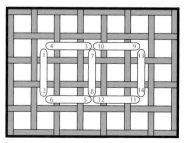

FOUR-SIDED STITCH

Demarest Adaptation Sampler

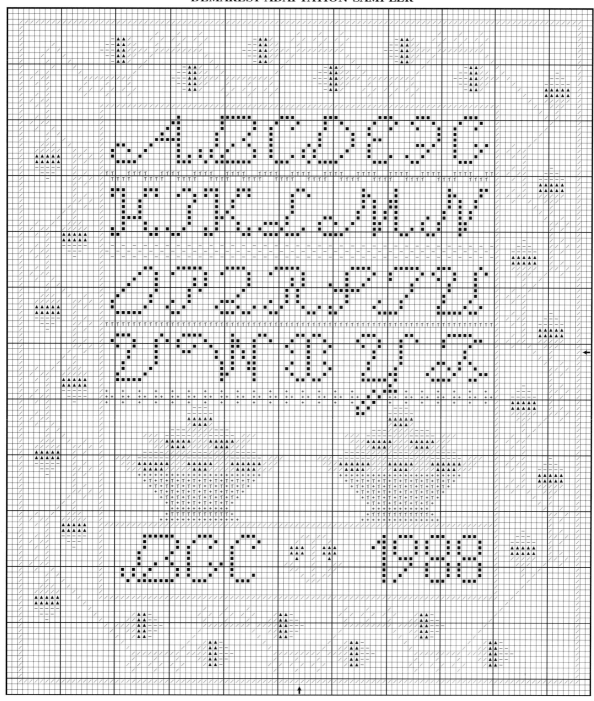

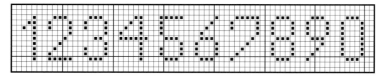

DMC	Coats	Anchor®	
−	758	3868	868	terra cotta, lt.
■	930	7052	922	antique blue, dk.
+	646	8500	273	beaver gray, dk.
T	841	5376	378	beige brown, lt.
∕	367	6018	217	pistachio green, dk.
▲	347	3013	1025	salmon, dk.

Fabric: 27-count cream linen

Stitch count: 120H x 104W
Design size:
14-count 8½" x 7½"
18-count 6¾" x 5¾"
22-count 5½" x 4¾"
27-count 8⅞" x 7¾"

Instructions: Cross stitch over two threads, using two strands of floss. Per-

sonalize using sampler alphabet. Work date using numerals chart.

NOTE: This design is an adaptation of an antique sampler completed by A. M. Demarest in 1834.

Adapted by Phyllis Hoffman

Each Day Is a Thread Sampler

Chart begins on page 82.

EACH DAY IS A THREAD SAMPLER

DMC Coats Anchor®

∕	501	6878	878	blue green, dk.
─	814	3044	44	garnet, dk.
·	841	5578	378	beige brown, lt.
❙	816	3410	20	garnet
○	932	7050	343	antique blue, lt.
✕	931	7051	921	antique blue, med.
■	500	6880	879	blue green, vy. dk.
+	729	2875	874	old gold, med.

Fabric: 27-count cream linen
Stitch count: 191H x 131W
Design size:
11-count 12" x 17½"
14-count 9½" x 13½"
18-count 7¼" x 10½"
22-count 6" x 8½"
27-count 14⅛" x 9¾"

Instructions: Cross stitch over two threads, using two strands of floss.

Designed by Phyllis Hoffman

Hands to Work Sampler

Chart begins on page 84.

EACH DAY IS A THREAD SAMPLER—TOP

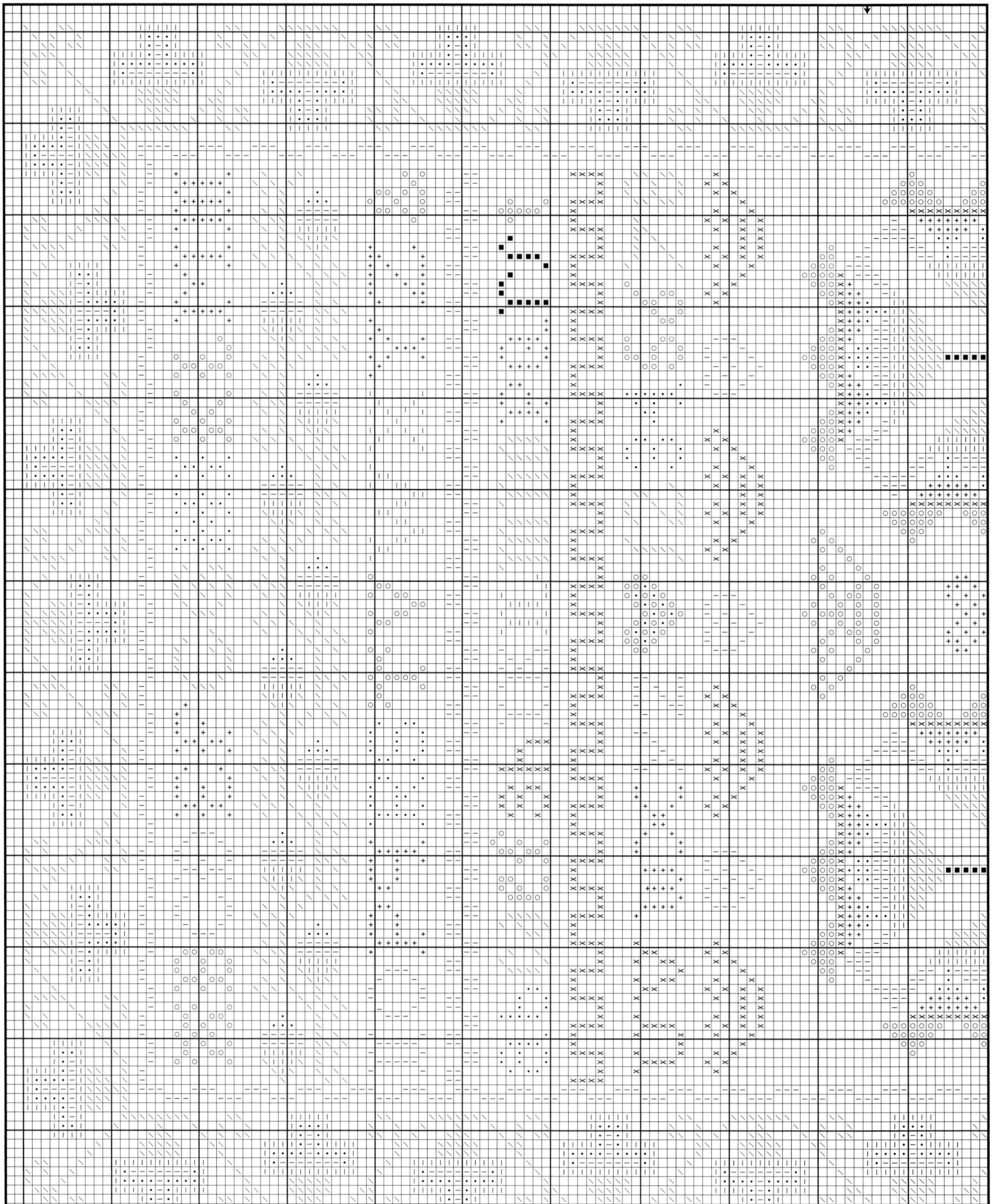

Shaded portion indicates overlap from previous page.

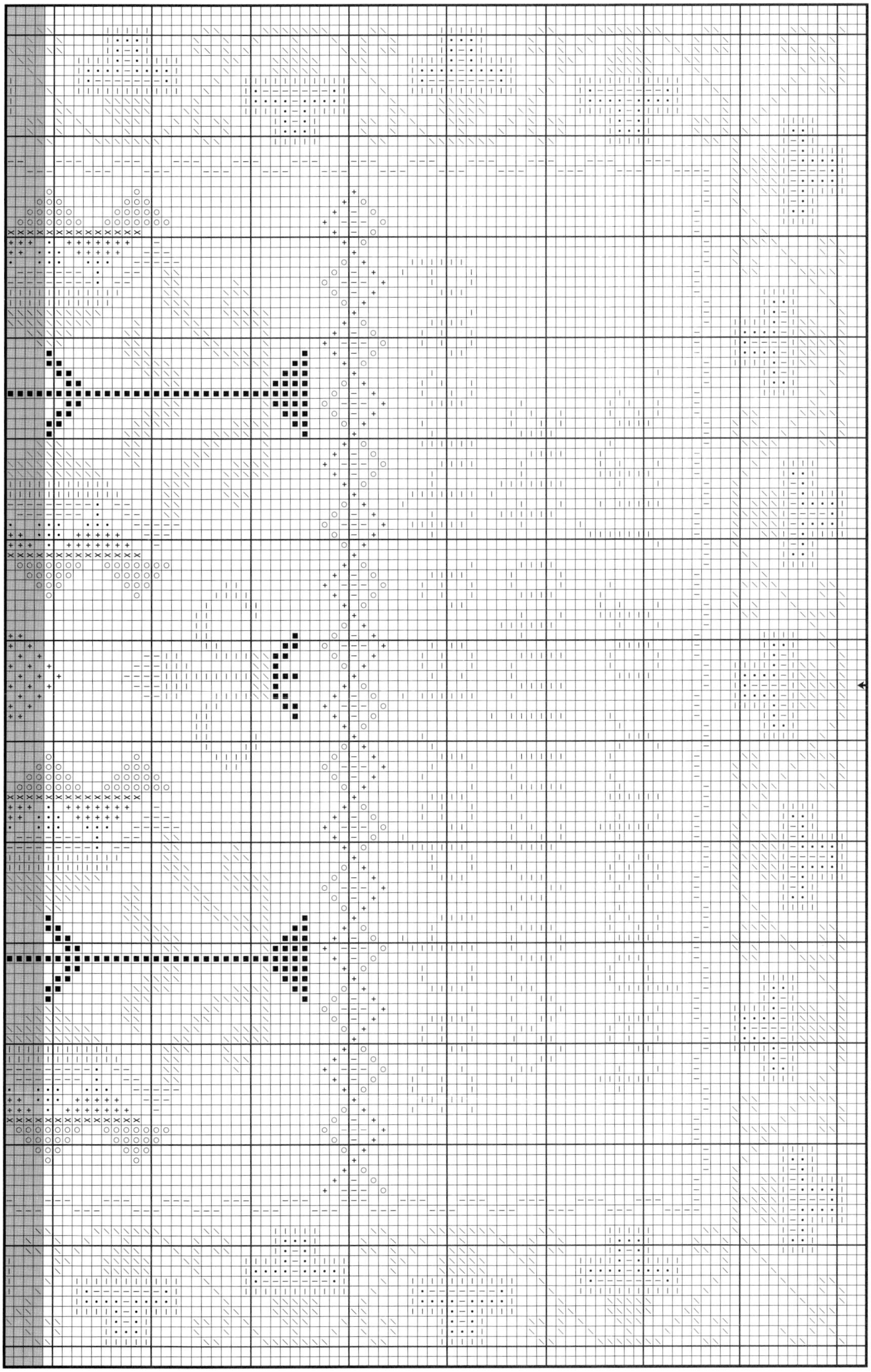

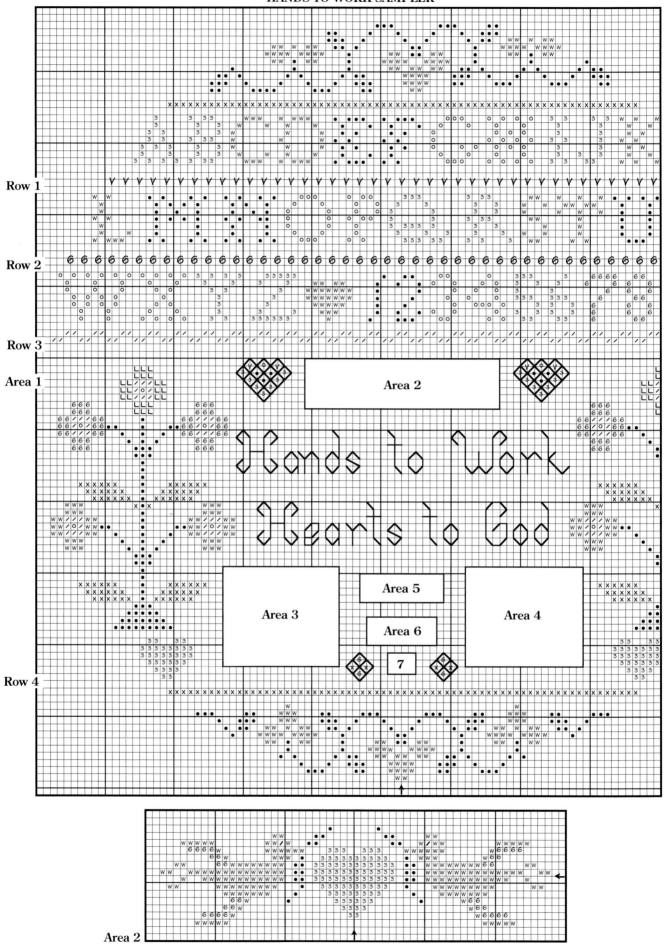

Shaded portion indicates overlap from previous page.

Area 3

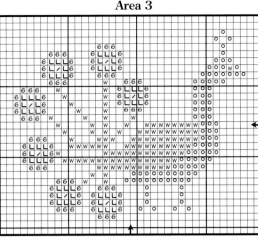

Area 4

Area 7

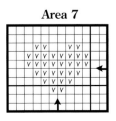

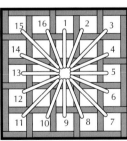

RICE STITCH

EYELET STITCH

QUEEN STITCH

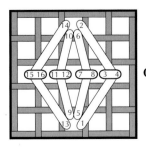

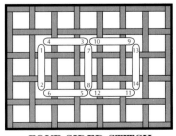

FOUR-SIDED STITCH

HANDS TO WORK SAMPLER

DMC Coats Anchor®

W 3768	—	779	gray-green, dk.
6 926	6007	850	gray-green, dk.
L 927	6006	848	gray-green, med.
• 520	6318	862	fern green, dk.
X 522	6316	860	fern green
○ 3045	2416	886	yellow-beige, dk.
⁄ 3046	2410	888	yellow-beige, med.
3 355	2339	5975	terra cotta, dk.
V 356	2975	9575	terra cotta, med.

Fabric: 27-count cream linen from Norden Crafts
Stitch count: 106H x 102W
Design size:
25-count 8½" x 8⅛"
27-count 7⅞" x 7⅝"
30-count 7⅛" x 6⅞"
32-count 6⅝" x 6⅜"

Instructions: Cross stitch over two threads, using two strands of floss unless otherwise indicated. Backstitch sentiment using two strands 355/2339/5975.

Special instructions:
Row 1: Work eyelet stitches using two strands 356/2975/9575.
Row 2: Work rice stitches using two strands 926/6007/850.
Row 3: Work four-sided stitches using two strands 3046/2410/888.
Area 1: Work queen stitches using two strands of color indicated.
Area 2: Center and cross stitch over one thread, using one strand of floss.
Area 3: Center and cross stitch over one thread, using one strand of floss.
Area 4: Center and cross stitch over one thread, using one strand of floss.
Area 5: Center and cross stitch initials, from sampler letters, over one thread using one strand 520/6318/862.
Area 6: Center and cross stitch date, from sampler numbers, over one thread using one strand 3768/—/799.
Area 7: Center and cross stitch over one thread, using one strand 356/2975/9575.
Row 4: Work queen stitches using two strands of color indicated.

Designed by Cathy Livingston

85

Neighbor's Blessings Sampler

NEIGHBOR'S BLESSINGS SAMPLER

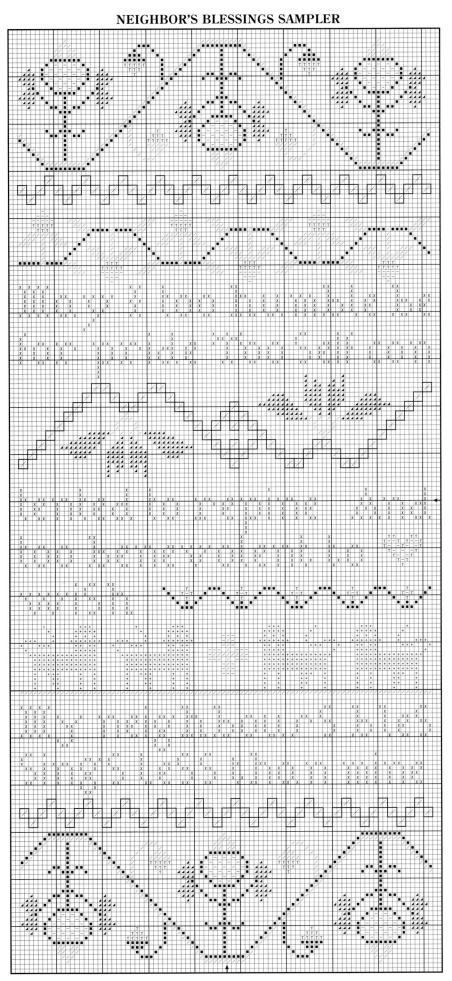

DMC Coats Anchor®

	DMC	Coats	Anchor	
-	3328	3071	10	salmon, med.
T	347	3013	1025	salmon, dk.
╱	3363	6317	262	pine green, med.
■	520	6318	862	fern green, dk.
▲	613	—	956	drab brown, lt.
+	610	5889	889	drab brown, vy. dk.
X	611	5898	898	drab brown, dk.

Fabric: 27-count unbleached linen from Norden Crafts, Inc.
Stitch count: 197H x 90W
Design size:
25-count 15⅞" x 7¼"
27-count 15" x 6 ¾"
28-count 14⅛" x 6½"
30-count 13¼" x 6"
32-count 12⅜" x 5⅝"
35-count 11¼" x 5¼

Instructions: Cross stitch over two threads, using two strands of floss. Work Algerian eye stitch for dividing bands where symbol ╱ appears over two squares.

Designed by Phyllis Hoffman

COFFEE BREAK

"Coffee Break" was created especially for the needleworker who has limited stitching time, or who simply enjoys her afternoon ritual of taking a few moments for her own enjoyment. The projects included in "Coffee Break" bring to the stitcher a variety of subjects and styles from which to choose. Achievable in just a few afternoons of pleasurable stitching, these designs will add fun and flair to your daily routine. From classic to whimsical, this assortment is certain to fill your afternoon coffee break with stitch after delightful stitch.

Above—*Day Lilies,* page 93; Left (clockwise from top left)—*Harvesttime,* page 90; *Sweets for the Sweet,* page 91; and *Did Someone Say Picnic?,* page 94.

COFFEE BREAK

Harvesttime

DMC	Coats	Anchor®	
/	970	2327	316 pumpkin, lt.
o	977	2306	313 golden brown, lt.
X	976	2308	309 golden brown, med.
●	801	5475	353 coffee brown, dk.
·	321	3500	47 Christmas red
+	304	3021	19 Christmas red, med.
◗	815	3000	22 garnet, med.
−	725	2298	305 topaz
V	783	5307	307 Christmas gold
\	733	—	280 olive green, med.
II	732	—	281 olive green
3	730	—	924 olive green, vy. dk.
I	470	6010	267 avocado green, lt.
C	469	6261	268 avocado green
Z	936	6269	269 avocado green, vy. dk.
6	610	5889	889 drab brown, vy. dk.
L	611	5898	898 drab brown, dk.
✳	898	5476	360 coffee brown, vy. dk.

Fabric: 26-count cream Sal-Em® Bread Cover from Carolina Cross Stitch, Inc.
Stitch count: 44H x 44W
Design size:
11-count 4" x 4"
14-count 3⅛" x 3⅛"
18-count 2⅜" x 2⅜"
26-count 3⅜" x 3⅜"

Instructions: Cross stitch over two threads, using two strands of floss. Backstitch using one strand of floss. Place large pumpkin and apple design in one corner. In remaining three corners, place single apple design.
NOTE: On 26-count Bread Cover, count in thirty **single** threads in direction of arrow to begin design.
Backstitch instructions: Backstitch in order listed.
Main design:

936	6269	269	three sets of leaves and stems on red apples
815	3000	22	lower-left red apple, lower-right red apple
783	5307	307	two yellow apples next to lower-left red apple
610	5889	889	top leaf
783	5307	307	top yellow apple
610	5889	889	lower-right leaf
783	5307	307	two yellow apples next to lower-right red apple
610	5889	889	leaf above lower-left red apple
730	—	924	pumpkin stem
801	5475	353	pumpkin
610	5889	889	lower center leaves

Single red apples in corners:

936	6269	269	apple leaves and stems
815	3000	22	apple

Designed by Cathy Livingston

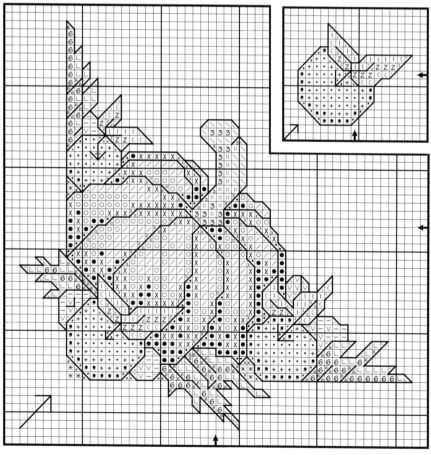

Sweets for the Sweet

DMC Coats Anchor®

X	223	3241	895	shell pink, med.
∕	224	3240	894	shell pink, lt.
c	3041	4222	871	antique violet, med.
−	677	—	886	old gold, vy. lt.
·	502	6876	877	blue green
bs	640	5393	393	beige-gray, vy. dk.

Fabric: 27-count ivory linen from Wichelt Imports, Inc.

Stitch count: 41H x 35W

Design size:
14-count 3" x 2½"
18-count 2¼" x 2"
27-count 3" x 2⅝"
30-count 2¾" x 2¼"

Instructions: Cross stitch over two threads, using two strands of floss. Backstitch using one strand of floss unless otherwise indicated.

Backstitch (bs) instructions:

502	6876	877	stems and leaves (two strands)
640	5393	393	remainder of backstitching

Designed by Robyn Taylor

Special Friends

DMC Coats Anchor®

o	502	6876	877	blue-green
X	760	3069	894	salmon
⁄	761	3068	893	salmon, lt.

Fabric: 25-count cream Dublin linen from Zweigart®
Stitch count: 55H x 111W
Design size:
14-count 4" x 8"
18-count 3⅛" x 6⅛"
25-count 4½" x 8⅞"
27-count 4⅛" x 8⅛"

Instructions: Cross stitch over two threads, using two strands of floss. Backstitch using two strands 502/6876/ 877.

Designed by Robyn Taylor

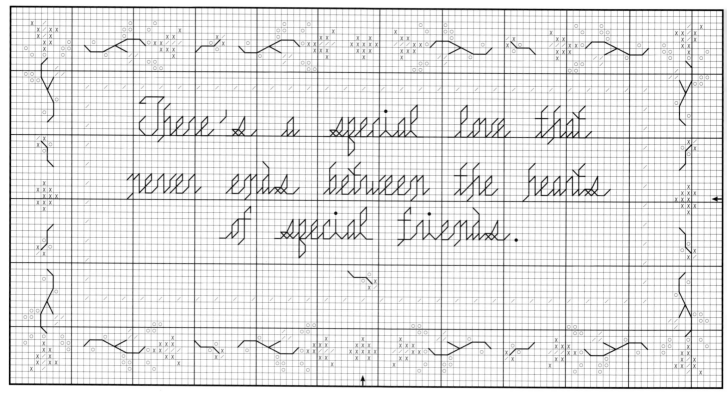

Day Lilies

DMC	Coats	Anchor®	
+	347	3013	13	salmon, dk.
o	351	3011	10	coral
∕	353	3006	8	peach flesh
=	356	2975	9575	terra cotta, med.
•	725	2298	305	topaz
X	758	3868	868	terra cotta, lt.
ı	772	6250	253	pine green, lt.
∅	632	5936	936	coffee brown, dk.
4	3051	6317	846	green-gray, dk.
3	3052	6316	860	green-gray, med.
2	3364	6010	843	pine green

Fabric: 25-count cream Lugana® from Zweigart®
Stitch count: 60H x 34W
Design size:
14-count 4¼" x 2½"
18-count 3⅜" x 1⅞"
25-count 4⅞" x 2¾"

Instructions: Cross stitch over two threads, using two strands of floss. Backstitch using one strand of floss.
Backstitch instructions:
353 3006 8 bud
347 3013 13 flower blooms
3051 6317 846 stems and leaves
632 5936 936 stamens

Designed by Teresa Wentzler

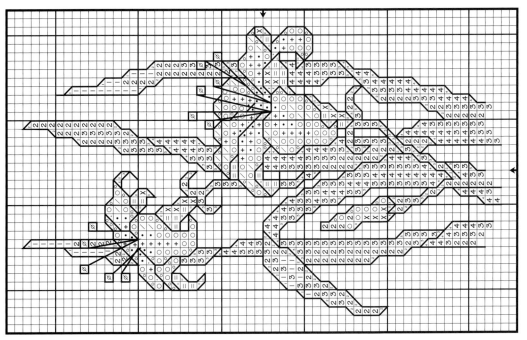

Did Someone Say Picnic?

DMC Coats Anchor®

C	645	8500	273	beaver gray, vy. dk.
∧	646	8500	273	beaver gray, dk.
∕	647	8900	8581	beaver gray, med.
-	738	5375	372	tan, vy. lt.
X	792	7150	177	cornflower, dk.
>	321	3500	47	red
o	304	3401	19	red, med.
\	white	1001	01	white
⋉	ecru	1002	387	ecru
✦	844	8501	382	beaver gray, ul. dk.

Fabric: 26-count cream Sal-Em® lace-edged place mat and napkin from Carolina Cross Stitch, Inc.

Stitch count:
Place Mat   47H x 95W
Napkin   22H x 12W

Design size:
Place Mat
14-count 3⅜" x 6⅞"
18-count 2⅝" x 5¼"
26-count 3⅝" x 7⅜"
30-count 3⅛" x 6⅜"
Napkin
14-count 1⅝" x ⅞"
18-count 1¼" x ⅝"
26-count 1¾" x 1"
30-count 1½" x ⅞"

Instructions: Cross stitch over two threads, using two strands of floss. Back-

stitch using one strand of floss unless otherwise indicated. Make French knots where symbol • appears at intersecting grid lines, using two strands of floss and wrapping floss around needle once.

NOTE: Work large design in lower-left corner of place mat, placing design edges ½" from fabric edges. Work small design in corner of napkin.

Backstitch instructions:

792	7150	177	lettering (two strands)
844	8501	382	arms, legs, hands, antennae, and smile (two strands), remainder of backstitching

French knot instructions:

white	1001	01	stars on flag, bandanna
844	8501	382	ends of antennae

Designed by Robyn Taylor

FRENCH KNOT

I Love Golf

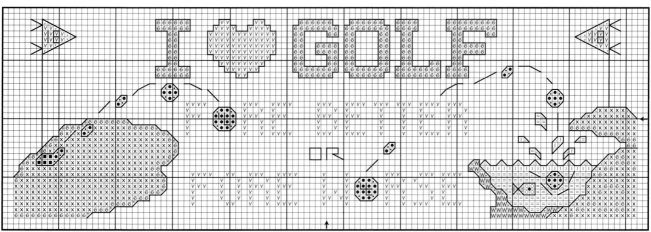

DMC	Coats	Anchor®	
6	904	6258	258	parrot green, vy. dk.
X	906	6256	256	parrot green, med.
V	349	2335	13	coral, dk.
o	971	2099	314	pumpkin
•	white	1001	01	white
■	310	8403	403	black
❘	3755	—	145	baby blue
=	334	7977	977	baby blue, med.
W	433	5471	944	brown, med.

Fabric: 28-count khaki Jobelan from Wichelt Imports, Inc.
Stitch count: 34H x 110W
Design size:
25-count 2¾" x 8⅞"
28-count 2½" x 7⅞"
30-count 2¼" x 7⅜"
32-count 2⅛" x 6⅞"

Instructions: Cross stitch over two threads, using two strands of floss.

Backstitch using one strand 310/8403/403. Make French knot for fish's eye where symbol • appears at intersecting grid lines, using two strands 310/8403/403 and wrapping floss around needle once.

Designed by Cathy Livingston

NURSERY RHYMES & HAPPY TIMES

Youngsters love cheery colors! This assortment of designs for babies and children, worked with bold primaries and gentle pastels, is guaranteed to make those of the younger set smile. From darling teddy bears to adorable cottontails, from a smiling airplane to lovable ducks and cute, green turtles, these charmers will make the children you know giggle with glee. Surprise a sister or close friend who has recently become a new mommy with a gift of your stitches for her wee one. Or sit down with your own children and let them choose their favorites for decorating their rooms.

Above—*Baby Treasures,* page 98; Left (clockwise from top left)—*Noah & His Ark,* page 104; *Summer Pleasures,* page 107; and *Brian's Room,* page 112.

Baby Treasures

Charts are on pages 99 and 100.

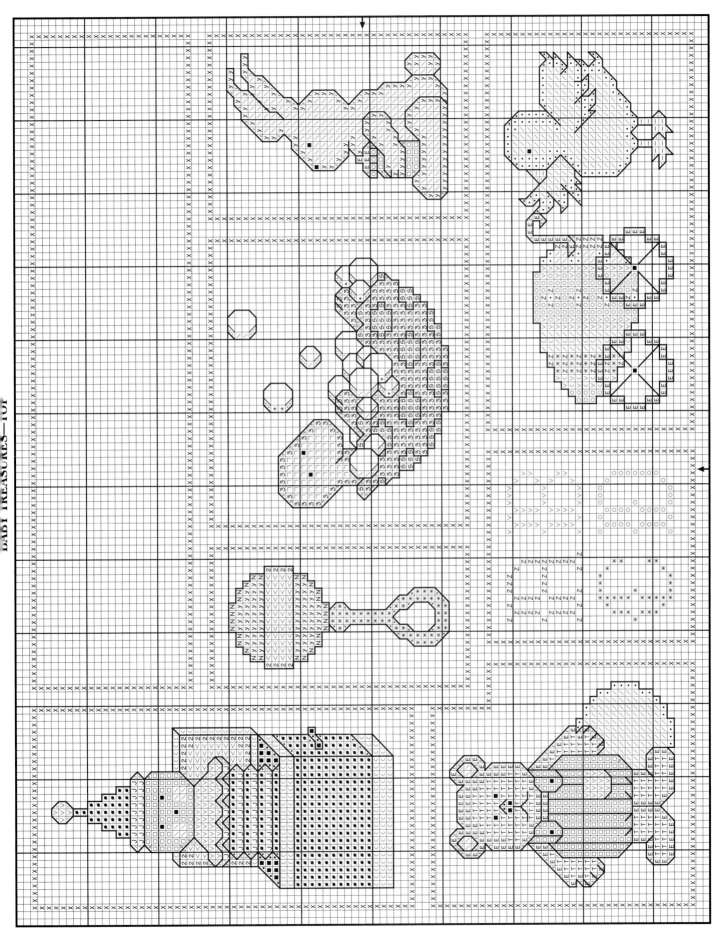

(Color code is on the next page)

BABY TREASURES

DMC	Coats	Anchor®	
□ white	1001	01	white
C 210	4303	108	lavender, med.
V 211	4303	342	lavender, lt.
S 320	6017	215	pistachio green, med.
X 334	7977	977	baby blue, med. (boy)
X 604	3001	66	cranberry, lt. (girl)
j 352	3008	9	coral, lt.
✗ 353	3006	8	peach flesh
3 368	6016	214	pistachio green, lt.
˥ 369	6015	260	pistachio green, vy. lt.
E 436	5943	362	tan
T 437	5942	361	tan, lt.
Z 605	—	60	cranberry, vy. lt.
- 741	2314	314	tangerine, med.
· 744	2293	301	yellow, pl.
/ 745	2296	300	yellow, lt. pl.
< 746	2275	275	off white
+ 775	7031	158	baby blue, lt.
y 776	3281	25	pink, med.
\ 818	3281	23	baby pink
2 822	5830	830	beige-gray, lt.
■ 844	8501	382	beaver gray, ul. dk.
o 955	6030	206	Nile green, lt.
✳ 3325	7976	144	baby blue
N 3326	3126	36	rose, lt.
bs 208	4301	111	lavender, vy. dk.
bs 317	8512	400	pewter gray

Fabric: 25-count Lugana from Zweigart® and 45H x 29W cream Anne cloth from Leisure Arts
Stitch count: 94H x 120W
Design size:
11-count 8⅝" x 11"
14-count 6¾" x 8⅝"
18-count 5¼" x 6⅝"
22-count 6¾" x 8⅝"
25-count 7½" x 9½"

Instructions: Cross stitch over two threads, using two strands of floss. Backstitch using one strand of floss. Use alphabet provided for personalization. **NOTE:** For a girl, stitch symbol X using 604/3001/66; for a boy, stitch symbol X using 334/7977/977. Backstitch girl's name using 604/3001/66. Backstitch boy's name using 334/7977/977.

Special instructions for afghan: Center desired designs in alternating squares. Cross stitch using four strands of floss. Backstitch using two strands of floss. Remove two threads from each woven strip, dividing afghan blocks. Weave ⅛"-wide ribbon, two over and three under, making sure ribbon is on top where borders intersect. Machine stitch around outer edge of entire afghan and fringe. Make small bows with ⅝"-wide ribbon and tack in empty squares.

Backstitch (bs) instructions:

844	8501	382	bear's nose and mouth, turtle and bubbles
208	4301	111	stripes on bear's pants
317	8512	400	remainder of back-stitching

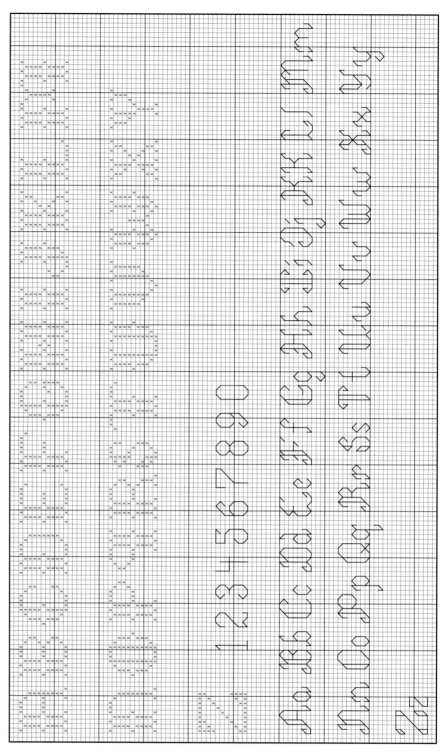

Ribbon colors:

Number	Color	Width	Yds.
640	lemon	⅝"	1
		⅛"	4
530	mint	⅝"	1
		⅛"	4
335	copen	⅝"	1
		⅛"	4
154	rose	⅝"	1
		⅛"	4

Designed by Robyn Taylor

Bunnies & Bears

Charts begin on page 102.

I LOVE RABBITS

DMC Coats Anchor®

●	930	7052	922	antique blue, dk.
W	931	7051	921	antique blue, med.
C	932	7050	343	antique blue, lt.
6	347	3013	13	salmon, dk.
+	3328	3071	10	salmon, med.
o	760	3069	894	salmon
-	761	3068	893	salmon, lt.
·	white	1001	01	white
■	310	8403	403	black
X	840	5379	379	beige-brown, med.
V	841	5376	378	beige-brown, lt.
∕	842	5933	376	beige-brown, vy. lt.
bs	838	5381	380	beige-brown, vy. dk.

Fabric: 14-count blue-gray Aida
Stitch count: 48H x103W
Design size:
11-count 4½" x 9½"
14-count 3½" x 7½"
18-count 2¾" x 5¾"
22-count 2¼" x 4¾"

Instructions: Cross stitch using two strands of floss. Backstitch using one strand of floss. Straight stitch whiskers using one strand 840/5379/379. Make French knots for buttons on rabbit's shirt, using two strands 347/3013/13 and wrapping floss around needle twice.
Backstitch (bs) instructions:
310 8403 403 eyes, eyebrows, lashes (each rabbit)
838 5381 380 remainder of backstitching

Designed by Cathy Livingston

I LOVE TEDDY BEARS

DMC Coats Anchor®

∕	739	5369	942	tan, ul. lt.
X	801	5475	353	coffee brown, dk.
C	433	5471	944	brown, med.
II	726	2295	295	topaz, lt.
V	725	2298	305	topaz
+	783	5307	307	Christmas gold
·	white	1001	01	white
■	310	8403	403	black
o	899	3282	38	rose, med.
-	3326	3126	36	rose, lt.
Z	349	2335	113	coral, dk.
=	350	3111	11	coral, med.
W	319	6246	246	pistachio green, vy. dk.
3	367	6018	210	pistachio green, dk.

I LOVE RABBITS

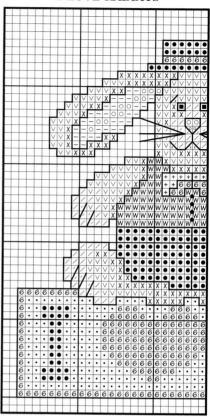

I LOVE TEDDY BEARS

Shaded portion indicates overlap from previous page.

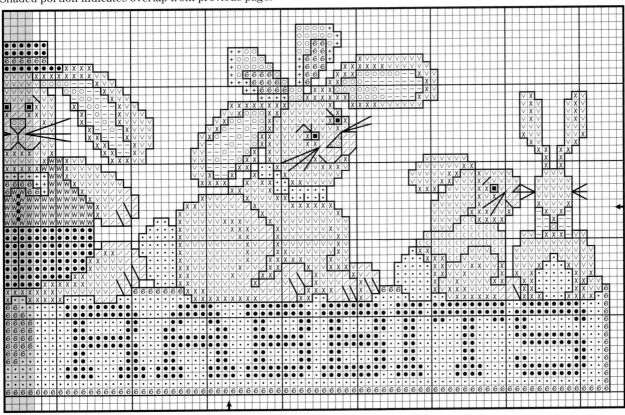

Shaded portion indicates overlap from previous page.

6 797 7023 132 royal blue
4 798 7022 131 delft, dk.
\ 799 7030 130 delft, med.
bs 3371 5478 382 black-brown

Fabric: 14-count Fiddler's Cloth from Charles Craft, Inc.
Stitch count: 57H x 143W
Design size:
11-count 5¼" x 13"
14-count 4" x 10¼"
18-count 3¼" x 8"
22-count 2½" x 6½"

Instructions: Cross stitch using two strands of floss. Backstitch using one strand of floss. Straight stitch using one strand of floss.

Backstitch (bs) instructions:
349 2335 13 lollipop handles
310 8403 403 eyes, noses, mouths, eyebrows, eyelashes, *HUNY* on jar, bee
3371 5478 382 remainder of backstitching

Straight stitch instructions:
798 7022 131 blue balloon strings
725 2298 305 yellow balloon strings
783 5307 307 piece of straw

Designed by Cathy Livingston

Noah & His Ark

DMC Coats Anchor®

9	349	2335	13	coral, dk.
⌐	444	2298	290	lemon, dk.
//	971	2099	314	pumpkin
⌐	988	6258	243	forest, med.
⊙	989	6266	242	forest
6	334	7977	977	baby blue, med.
ε	333	—	119	blue violet, dk.
◢	986	6021	246	forest, vy. dk.
∧	987	6258	244	forest, dk.
■	310	8403	403	black
▲	838	5381	380	beige-brown, vy. dk.
w	839	5360	360	beige-brown, dk.
*	920	3337	339	copper, med.
↙	921	—	349	copper
◗	355	2339	5975	terra cotta, dk.
3	782	5308	308	topaz, med.
o	783	5307	307	gold
+	680	2876	907	old gold, dk.
‖	420	5374	374	hazelnut, dk.
c	353	3006	8	peach flesh
∣	948	2331	778	peach flesh, vy. lt.
8	976	2308	309	gold brown, med.
V	977	2306	313	gold brown, lt.
≠	975	5349	355	gold brown, dk.
5	414	8513	235	steel gray, dk.
·	white	1001	01	white
=	762	8510	397	pearl gray, vy. lt.
T	993	6185	185	aqua, lt.
G	992	6186	187	aqua
N	924	6008	851	gray-green, vy. dk.
⟍	927	6006	848	gray-green, med.
>	928	7225	274	gray-green, lt.
∴	307	2290	289	lemon
∪	842	5933	376	beige-brown, vy. lt.
⸫	ecru	1002	387	ecru
2	841	5578	378	beige-brown, vy. lt.
z	844	8501	382	beaver gray, ul. dk.
X	646	8500	273	beaver gray, dk.
∩	647	8900	8581	beaver gray, med.
◤	3021	5395	273	brown-gray, dk.
\	739	5369	942	tan, ul. lt.
−	738	5375	372	tan, vy. lt.
M	434	5000	370	brown, lt.
♥	433	5471	944	brown, med.
/	3325	7976	144	baby blue
●	312	7979	979	navy, lt.
bs	926	6007	850	gray-green, dk.

Fabric: 28-count khaki Annabelle from Zweigart®

Stitch count: 172H x 136W

Design size:

14-count 12¼" x 9¾"
18-count 9½" x 7½"
28-count 12¼" x 9¾"
32-count 10¾" x 8½"

Instructions: Cross stitch over two threads, using two strands of floss. Backstitch using one strand of floss unless otherwise indicated. Make French knots using two strands of floss, wrapping floss around needle twice. Make Straight stitches for the sun's rays using one strand 444/2298/290.

Backstitch (bs) instructions:

414	8513	235	doves, mice, outer edges of head covering on Mr. and Mrs. Noah, Noah's eyes and nose
310	8404	403	lettering (two strands), penguin beaks, line between cats
926	6007	850	storm cloud, raindrops
975	5349	355	Noah's robe
927	6006	848	sun cloud
986	6021	246	Mrs. Noah's robe
838	5381	380	line under Ark's roof, door, hinges, ramp
924	6008	851	fish
839	5360	360	rabbits, Mrs. Noah's eyes and nose
841	5578	378	sheep
3021	5395	273	cats, elephants
647	8900	8581	breast of each penguin
433	5471	944	giraffe's tails, ears, and eyes
844	8501	382	ducks (**except** feet)
971	2099	314	ducks' feet (two strands)

French knots:

414	8513	235	doves' eyes
924	6008	851	fishes' eyes
844	8501	382	ducks' eyes
839	5360	360	rabbits' eyes, sheeps' eyes
3021	5395	273	giraffes' eyes, penguins' eyes
353	3006	8	rabbits' noses

Designed by Cathy Livingston

NOAH & HIS ARK—TOP

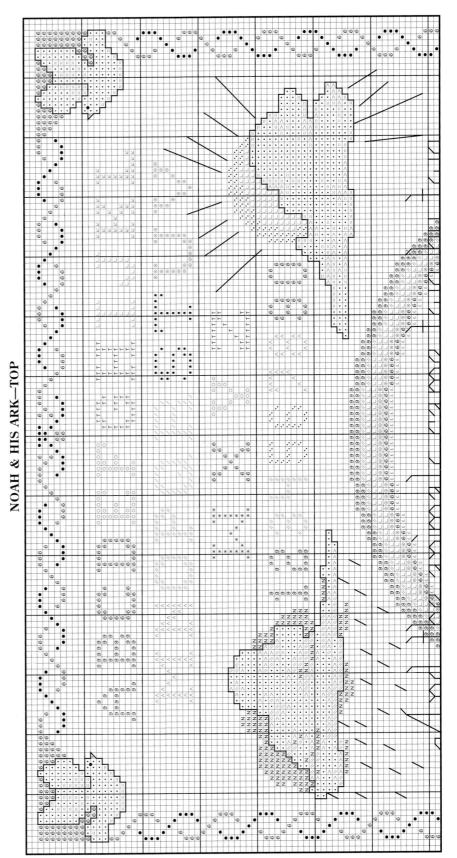

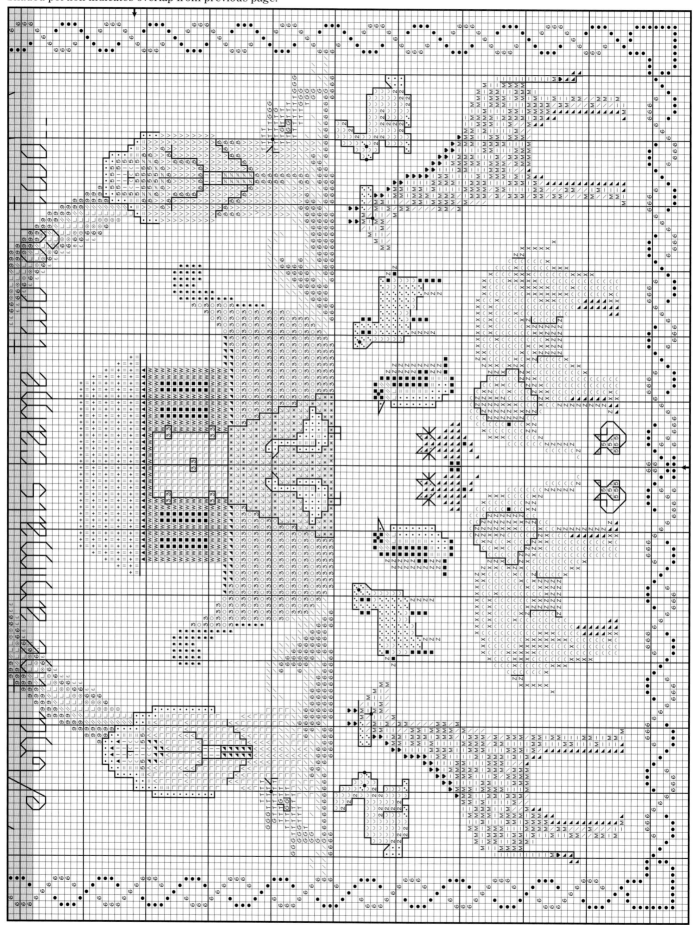

Summer Pleasures

Charts begin on page 108.

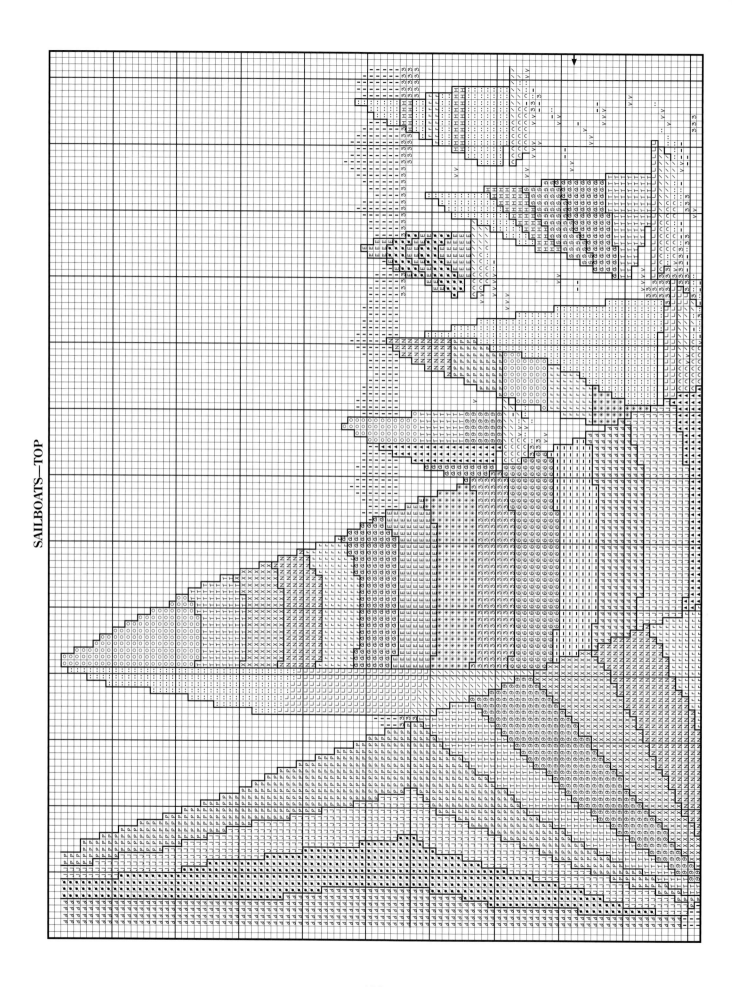

SAILBOATS

	DMC	Coats	Anchor®	
I	341	7005	117	blue-violet, lt.
S	806	7169	169	peacock, dk.
L	762	8510	397	pearl gray, vy. lt.
a	321	3500	47	red
✗	943	6187	188	aqua, med.
··	white	1001	01	white
3	3766	—	—	peacock, lt.
6	3765	—	170	peacock, vy. lt.
9	444	2298	290	lemon, dk.
*	333	—	119	blue-violet, dk.
d	958	6186	187	sea green, dk.
J	703	6238	238	chartreuse
P	701	6226	227	green, lt.
T	307	2290	289	lemon
X	741	2314	314	tangerine, med.
N	740	2099	316	tangerine
r	666	3046	46	red, bt.
H	816	3410	20	garnet
╱	415	8398	398	pearl gray
∩	318	8511	399	steel gray, lt.
-	959	6186	186	sea green, med.
▲	699	6228	923	green
o	445	2288	288	lemon, lt.
E	340	7110	118	blue-violet, med.
V	807	7168	168	peacock
bs	310	8403	403	black

Fabric: 28-count ice blue Annabelle from Zweigart®
Stitch count: 160H x 130W
Design size:
14-count 11½" x 9¼"
18-count 8⅞" x 7¼"
25-count 12⅞" x 10⅜"
28-count 11½" x 9¼"

Instructions: Cross stitch over two threads, using two strands of floss. Backstitch (bs) using one strand 310/ 8403/403.

Designed by Charlotte Holder

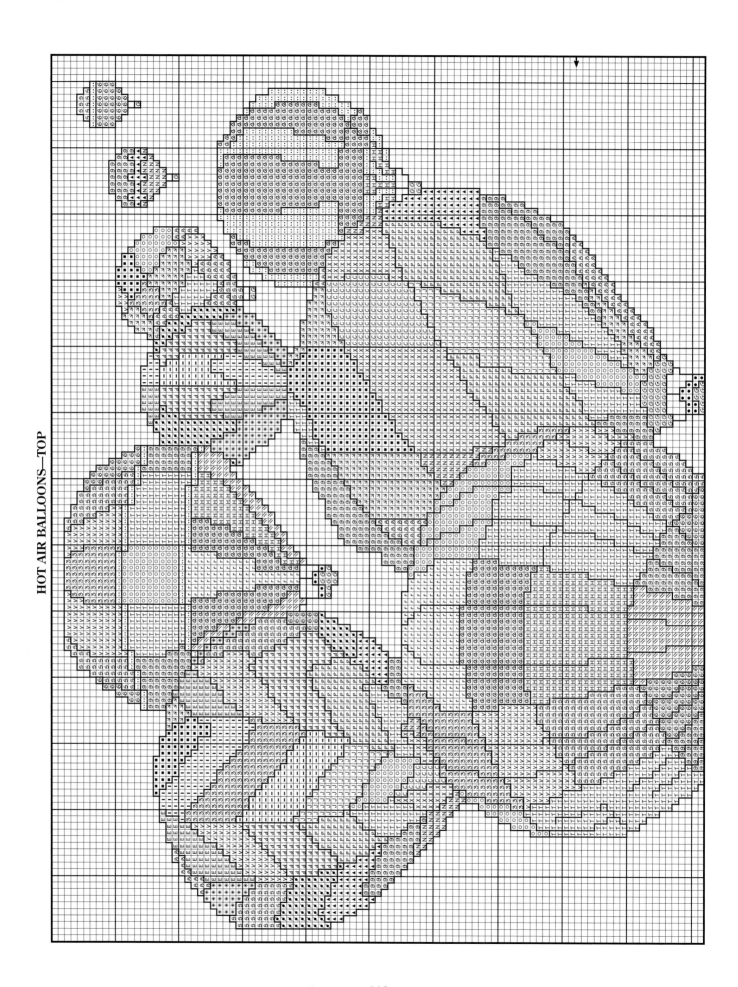

Shaded portion indicates overlap from previous page.

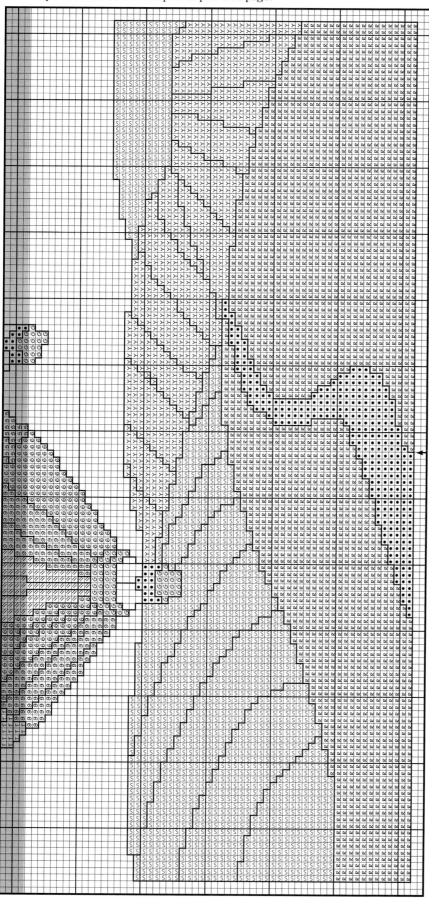

HOT AIR BALLOONS

DMC Coats Anchor®

	DMC	Coats	Anchor®	
a	321	3500	47	red
o	445	2288	288	lemon, lt.
r	666	3046	46	red, bt.
H	816	3410	20	garnet
T	307	2290	289	lemon
I	341	7005	117	blue-violet, lt.
3	3766	—	—	peacock, lt.
6	3765	—	170	peacock, vy. dk.
9	444	2298	290	lemon, dk.
8	600	3056	59	cranberry, vy. dk.
\	814	3044	44	garnet, dk.
··	white	1001	01	white
▲	699	6228	923	green
✎	943	6187	188	aqua, med.
↘	602	3063	63	cranberry, med.
■	603	3001	62	cranberry
−	959	6186	186	sea green, med.
✳	333	—	119	blue-violet, dk.
N	740	2099	316	tangerine
P	701	6226	227	green, lt.
x	741	2314	314	tangerine, med.
E	340	7110	118	blue-violet, med.
d	958	6186	187	sea green, dk.
S	806	7169	169	peacock, dk.
v	807	7168	168	peacock
J	703	6238	238	chartreuse
C	742	2303	303	tangerine, lt.
G	433	5471	944	brown, med.
·	436	5943	362	tan
R	469	6261	268	avocado
Y	471	6010	266	avocado, vy. lt.
∽	472	6253	264	avocado, ul. lt.
bs	310	8404	403	black

Fabric: 28-count ice blue Annabelle from Zweigart®
Stitch count: 160H x 130W
Design size:

14-count	11½" x 9¼"
18-count	8⅞" x 7¼"
25-count	12⅞" x 10⅜"
28-count	11½" x 9¼"

Instructions: Cross stitch over two threads, using two strands of floss. Backstitch using one strand of floss.
Backstitch (bs) instructions:
433 5471 944 land
310 8404 403 remainder of back-stitching

Designed by Charlotte Holder

Brian's Room

Charts are on page 113.

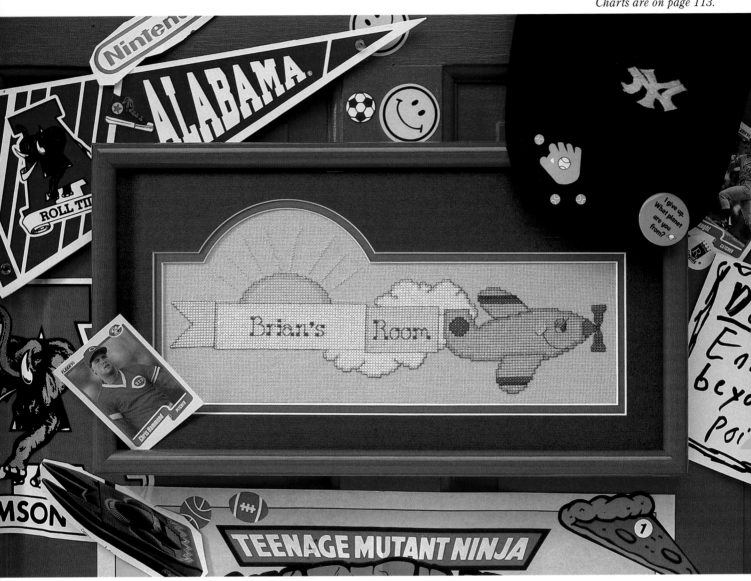

	DMC	Coats	Anchor®	
c	725	2298	305	topaz
−	726	2294	295	topaz, lt.
e	822	—	830	beige-gray, lt.
∧	644	—	831	beige-gray, med.
·	746	—	275	off white
6	798	7022	131	delft, dk.
z	800	7021	144	delft, pl.
⁄	white	1001	01	white
X	318	8511	399	steel gray, lt.
I	415	8510	399	pearl gray
7	797	7023	132	royal blue
∴	700	6227	228	green, bt.
■	535	8400	273	ash gray, vy. lt.

+	317	8512	400	pewter gray
3	350	3011	11	coral, med.
o	349	2335	13	coral, dk.
∩	353	3006	8	peach flesh

Fabric: 25-count pewter Lugana® from Zweigart®
Stitch count: 61H x 157W
Design size:

14-count 4⅜" x 11¼"
18-count 3⅜" x 8¾"
22-count 2¾" x 7⅛"
25-count 4¾" x12½"

Instructions: Cross stitch over two threads, using two strands of floss. Backstitch using one strand of floss unless otherwise indicated.

Backstitch instructions:

725	2298	305	sun's rays (two strands)
798	7022	131	*Brian's Room* (two strands)
535	8400	273	remainder of backstitching

Designed by Robyn Taylor

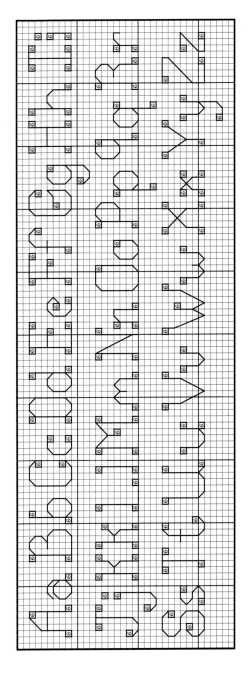

HOLIDAY STITCHERY

*H*olidays are a great reason to stitch! Thanksgiving, Christmas, Easter, or the Fourth of July—needlework marks each special day and season in a way all its own, providing its maker with a unique, personal way to decorate her home and with one-of-a-kind gifts for friends and family. From simple to ornate, from traditional to unexpected, from the pretty pastels of Easter to the colors and motifs of the Christmas season, these designs are certain to become valued family heirlooms.

Above—*Bountiful Harvest,* page 117; Left (clockwise from top left)—*Heralding Angel,* page 116; *Ol' Kriss Kringle,* page 122; and *Happy Easter,* page 137.

Heralding Angel

Chart begins on page 118.

Bountiful Harvest

Chart begins on page 120.

HERALDING ANGEL

DMC Coats Anchor®

- •⌈ 500 6880 879 blue-green, vy. dk.
  ⌊ 085BF Kreinik   peacock
                     (four spools)
- 6⌈ 501 6878 878 blue-green, dk.
  ⌊ 085BF Kreinik   peacock
- X⌈ 502 6876 877 blue-green
  ⌊ 085BF Kreinik   peacock
- ∧⌈ 503 6879 876 blue-green, med.
  ⌊ 002BF Kreinik   gold (three
                     spools)
- ⌐⌈ 504 6875 875 blue-green, lt.
  ⌊ 002BF Kreinik   gold
- o⌈ 746 2275 275 off-white
  ⌊ 002BF Kreinik   gold
- ı⌈ 677 — 886 old gold, vy. lt.
  ⌊ 002BF Kreinik   gold
- =⌈ 676 2874 887 old gold, lt.
  ⌊ 002BF Kreinik   gold
- V⌈ 729 2875 874 old gold, med.
  ⌊ 002BF Kreinik   gold
- · 948 2331 778 peach flesh, vy. lt.
- - 950 2336 376 sportsman flesh
- ⊙ 754 2331 5 peach flesh, lt.
- 3 433 5471 944 brown, med.
- C 434 5000 370 brown, lt.
- L 435 5371 363 brown, vy. lt.
- ⁄ 002HL Kreinik   gold (hs)
- bs 680 2876 907 old gold, dk.
- bs 801 5475 353 coffee brown, dk.
- bs 407 — 887 sportsman
                flesh, dk.

801 5475 353 hair
500 6880 879 gown (including where
             gown meets wings)
680 2876 907 wings [line separating
             wings—two strands; re-
             mainder of wings
             (outer edges only)—
             one strand]

002HL Kreinik   star's rope (two strands)

Designed by Cathy Livingston

Fabric: 25-count moss green Lugana from Zweigart®
Stitch count: 140H x 163W
Design size:
14-count 10" x 11¾"
18-count 7¾" x 9"
25-count 11¼" x 13"
27-count 10 ⅜" x12⅛"
28-count 10" x 11¾"
30-count 9¼" x 11"
32-count 8⅝" x 10⅛"
35-count 8" x 9⅜"

Instructions: Cross stitch over two threads, using two strands of floss. When floss color and Kreinik Metallics are bracketed together, use one strand of floss and two strands of Kreinik Blending Filament. Backstitch using one strand of floss unless otherwise indicated. Make half stitches (hs) using two strands 002HL.

Backstitch (bs) instructions:
Backstitch in order listed.
503 6879 876 sash, trim on sleeves
407 — 887 left side of face, chin,
          neck, hands
435 5371 363 eyes, nose, edge of ear

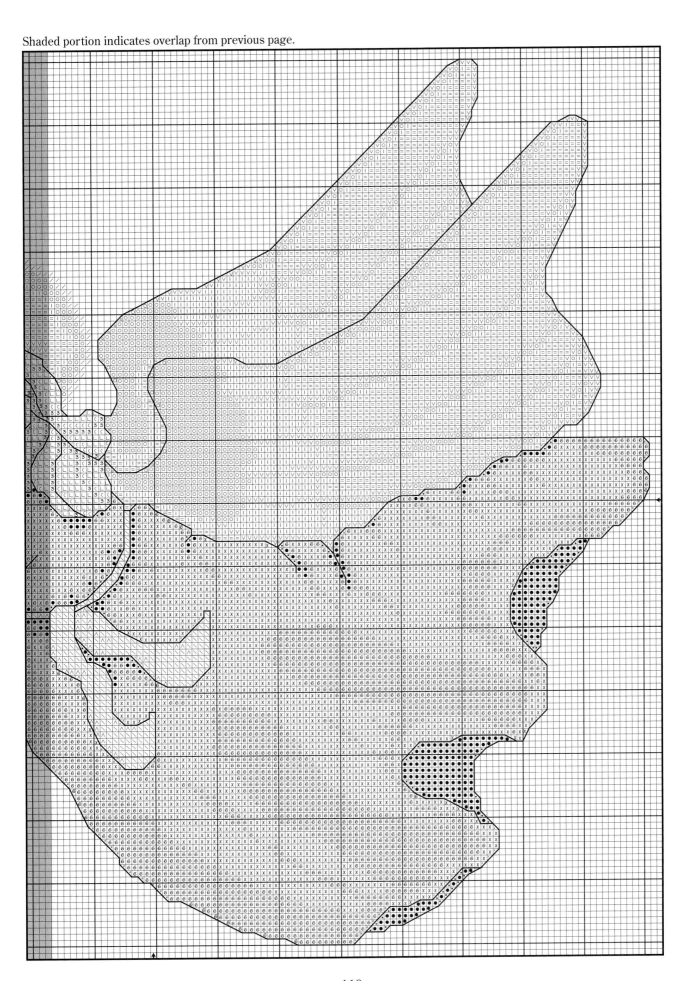

BOUNTIFUL HARVEST

DMC Coats Anchor®

	DMC	Coats	Anchor®	
-	738	5375	373	tan, vy. lt.
∪	437	5942	361	tan, lt.
✱	434	5000	370	brown, lt.
∴	722	2323	323	orange spice, lt.
↘	721	2324	324	orange spice, med.
H	720	2322	32	orange spice, dk.
W	937	6268	268	avocado green, med.
✐	470	6010	267	avocado green, lt.
‖	321	3500	47	Christmas red
<	498	3410	43	Christmas red, vy. dk.
ε	815	3000	22	garnet, med.
·ǀ· [	727	2289	293	topaz, vy. lt.
	472	6253	264	avocado green, ul. lt.
∧	472	6253	264	avocado green, ul. lt.
9	471	6010	266	avocado green, vy. lt.
T	727	2289	293	topaz, vy. lt.
8 [	730	—	924	olive green, vy. dk.
	830	—	277	golden olive, dk.
4	733	—	280	olive green, med.
7	734	—	279	olive green, lt.
L	741	2314	314	tangerine, med.
○	977	2306	313	golden brown, lt.
5	976	2308	309	golden brown, med.
M	3011	6845	845	khaki green, dk.
2	3012	6843	844	khaki green, med.
≠	3013	6842	842	khaki green, lt.
6 [	915	—	89	plum, dk.
	550	4107	102	violet, vy. dk.
> [	917	4089	88	plum, med.
	552	4092	101	violet, med.
⊃ [	718	—	88	plum
	554	4104	96	violet, lt.

BOUNTIFUL HARVEST

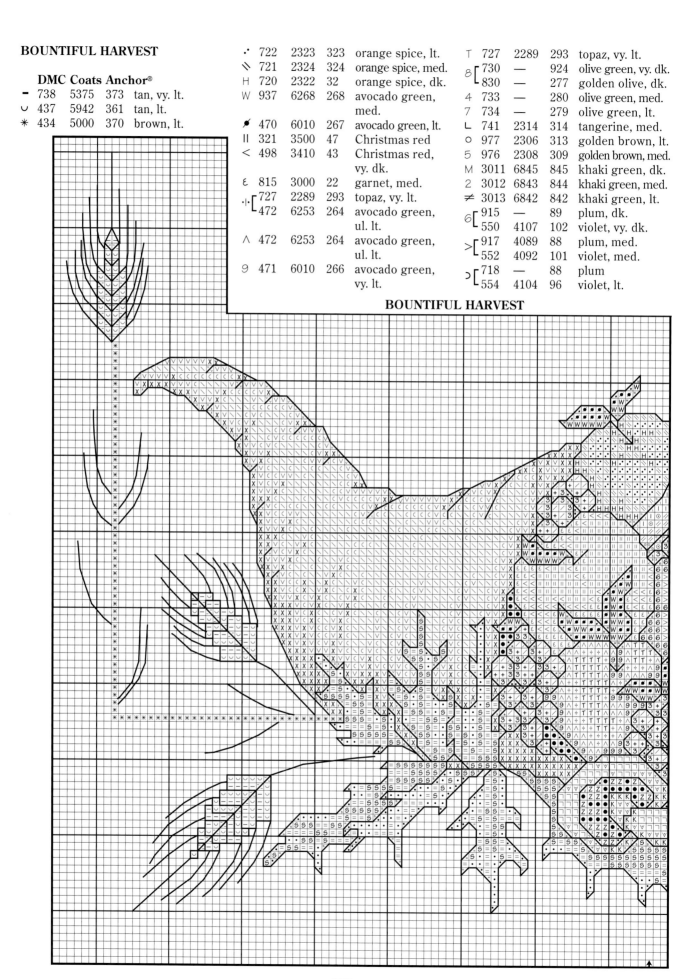

3	550	4107	102	violet, vy. dk.
+	552	4092	101	violet, med.
/	554	4104	96	violet, lt.
⌐	822	5830	830	beige gray, lt.
V⌈	644	5831	831	beige gray, med.
⌊	642	5832	832	beige gray, dk.
K	640	5393	393	beige gray, vy. dk.
Z	3021	5395	273	brown gray, vy. dk.
●	310	8403	403	black
//	725	2298	305	topaz
❘	743	2302	302	yellow, med.
N	611	5898	898	drab brown, dk.
⊙	612	—	832	drab brown, med.
S	898	5476	360	coffee brown, vy. dk.
=	300	—	352	mahogany, vy. dk.
·	301	—	349	mahogany, med.

X	420	5374	374	hazelnut, dk.
V	680	2876	907	old gold, dk.
C	729	2875	874	old gold, med.
\	676	2874	887	old gold, lt.
bs	435	5371	363	brown, vy. lt.

Fabric: 25-count cream Dublin linen from Zweigart®
Stitch count: 104H x 160W
Design size:
11-count 9½" x 14⅝"
14-count 7½" x 11½"
18-count 5⅞" x 8⅞"
22-count 4¾" x 7⅜"
25-count 8¼" x 12¾"

Instructions: Cross stitch over two threads, using three strands of floss. Backstitch using one strand of floss. Straight stitch using one strand of floss.

Backstitch (bs) instructions:
Backstitch in order listed.
640 5393 393 bottom mushroom **except** base, two mushrooms below pear **except** bases

310	8403	403	base of bottom mushroom, bases of mushrooms below pear
550	4107	102	all grapes **except** bottom of bunch between bananas
730	—	924	pear
815	3000	22	small and large red apples
3011	6845	845	pumpkin stem
301	—	349	pumpkin
471	6010	266	yellow-green apple
612	—	832	bananas
720	2322	32	peach
915	—	89	plum
937	6268	268	green leaves and stems on **all** fruit
898	5476	360	all autumn leaves
420	5374	374	basket
435	5371	363	wheat centers

Straight stitch instructions:
435 5371 363 straight lines around wheat, placed randomly

Designed by Cathy Livingston

Shaded portion indicates overlap from previous page.

Ol' Kriss Kringle

Chart begins on page 124.

DMC Coats Anchor®

Symbol	DMC	Coats	Anchor®	Color
·	white	1001	01	white (two skeins)
=	415	8398	398	pearl gray
⌀	318	8511	399	steel gray, lt.
▲	414	8513	235	steel gray, dk.
◁	647	8900	8581	beaver gray, vy. dk.
★	646	8500	273	beaver gray, med.
◤	844	8501	382	beaver gray, ul. dk.
■	310	8403	403	black
‖	676	2874	887	old gold, lt.
⊙	729	2875	874	old gold, med.
⌐	435	5371	363	brown, vy. lt.
⊿	783	5307	307	gold
✕	434	5000	370	brown, lt.
◣	433	5471	944	brown, med.
▼	801	5475	353	coffee, dk.
⊷	3371	5478	382	black-brown
9	400	5349	351	mahogany, dk.
Φ	304	3401	19	red, med.
●	816	3410	20	garnet
✖	815	3000	22	garnet, med.
ε	760	3069	894	salmon
∍	3328	3071	10	salmon, med.
⌐	948	2331	778	peach flesh, vy. lt.
⌐	3779	3868	4146	terra cotta, ul. vy. lt.
∇	3778	2338	9575	terra cotta, lt.
ɑ	356	2975	9575	terra cotta, med.
✗	3777	2339	1015	terra cotta, vy. dk.
··	932	7050	343	antique blue, lt.
+	931	7051	921	antique blue, med.
◇	930	7052	922	antique blue, dk.
#	3750	—	1036	antique blue, vy. lt.
⊥	799	7030	130	delft, med.
A	797	7023	132	royal blue
↗	445	2288	288	lemon, lt.
⦻	444	2298	290	lemon, dk.
✳	900	2329	333	burnt orange, dk.
4	971	2099	314	pumpkin
<	320	6017	215	pistachio, med.
∩	367	6018	210	pistachio, dk.
∧	319	6246	246	pistachio, vy. dk.
⊗	890	6021	212	green, dk.
M	911	6205	205	emerald, lt.
z	909	6228	230	emerald, med.
♦	[445	2288	288	lemon, lt.
	032BF	Kreinik		pearl]
/	[white	1001	01	white
	032BF	Kreinik		pearl]
o	[3328	3071	10	salmon, med.
	304	3401	19	red, med.]
◖	[304	3401	19	red, med.
	816	3410	20	garnet]
X	[911	6205	205	emerald, lt.
	367	6018	210	pistachio, dk.]
◕	[319	6246	246	pistachio, vy. dk.
	909	6228	230	emerald, med.]
e	[032BF	Kreinik		pearl
	3753	7031	128	antique blue, ul. vy. lt.]

Symbol	DMC	Coats	Anchor®	Color
✗	[400	5349	351	mahogany, dk.
	3777	2339	1015	terra cotta, vy. dk.]
◹	[400	5349	351	mahogany, dk.
	3328	3071	10	salmon, med.]
8	[3777	2339	1015	terra cotta, vy. dk.
	3778	2338	9575	terra cotta, lt.]
Z	[932	7050	343	antique blue, lt.
	032BF	Kreinik		pearl]
◤	[318	8511	399	steel gray, lt.
	932	7050	343	antique blue, lt.]
V	[415	8398	398	pearl gray
	3753	7031	128	antique blue, ul. vy. lt.]
⊂	[948	2331	778	peach flesh, vy. lt.
	3779	3868	4146	terra cotta, ul. vy. lt.]
⊖	[3779	3868	4146	terra cotta, ul. vy. lt.
	3778	2338	9575	terra cotta, lt.]
÷	[white	1001	01	white (two skeins)
	647	8900	8581	beaver gray, vy. dk.]
⊐	[647	8900	8581	beaver gray, vy. dk.
	646	8500	273	beaver gray, med.]
B	[646	8500	273	beaver gray, med.
	844	8501	382	beaver gray, ul. dk.]
V	[932	7050	343	antique blue, lt.
	931	7051	921	antique blue, med.]
♡	[931	7051	921	antique blue, med.
	930	7052	922	antique blue, dk.]
W	[930	7052	922	antique blue, dk.
	3750	—	1036	antique blue, vy. dk.]
bs	355	2339	5975	terra cotta, dk.
bs	Metallic Thread			gold

Fabric: 28-count misty blue Quaker Cloth from Zweigart®
Stitch count: 162H x 125W
Design size:
25-count 13" x10"
28-count 11⅝" x 9"
30-count 10⅞" x 8⅜"
32-count 10⅛" x 7⅞"

Instructions: Cross stitch over two threads, using two strands of floss. Backstitch using one strand of floss unless otherwise indicated. Make French knots where ● appears at intersecting grid lines, using two strands of floss and wrapping floss around needle once. When two colors are bracketed together, use one strand of each. When floss color and Kreinik Metallics are bracketed together, use one strand of each.

Backstitch (bs) instructions:
white 1001 01 candles in windows, Santa's belt buckle, curtains in top window of green house, outer edge of chimney
932 7050 343 snow on rooftops
890 6021 212 Santa's gloves, Christ-mas tree in green house, bear's bow tie, outer borderline (two strands)
310 8403 403 black edge of Santa's boot
3371 5478 382 windowpanes, sides of Santa's boot, rims of Santa's eyes, Santa's belt, bear's mouth, bear's nose, train (except wheels)
844 8501 382 opening of toy bag in Santa's hand, top opening of toy bag around toys
801 5475 353 remainder of toy bag, brown part of sole on Santa's boot
3750 — 1036 blue part of boat
414 8513 235 remainder of boat, white fur on Santa's suit, inside edge of chimney, train wheels
815 3000 22 red parts of Santa's suit
816 3410 20 red part of block beside bear, inner borderline
646 8500 273 Santa's beard, Santa's moustache, Santa's eyebrows
356 2975 9575 Santa's nostrils
355 2339 5975 Santa's eyelids, wrinkles around Santa's eyes
3778 2338 9575 doll's face, doll's arms
900 2329 333 doll's hair
400 5349 351 trumpet
797 7023 132 blue parts of doll's dress
434 5000 370 remainder of bear
367 6018 210 green side of block beside bear
445 2288 288 yellow side of block beside bear
444 2298 290 yellow side of block beside doll
318 8511 399 blue-and-white ball
Metallic Thread middle borderline

French knot instructions:
971 2099 314 candle flames in windows
3371 5478 382 doll's eyes

Designed by Angela Pullen

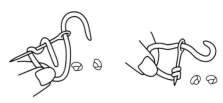

FRENCH KNOT

OL' KRISS KRINGLE—TOP

Shaded portion indicates overlap from previous page.

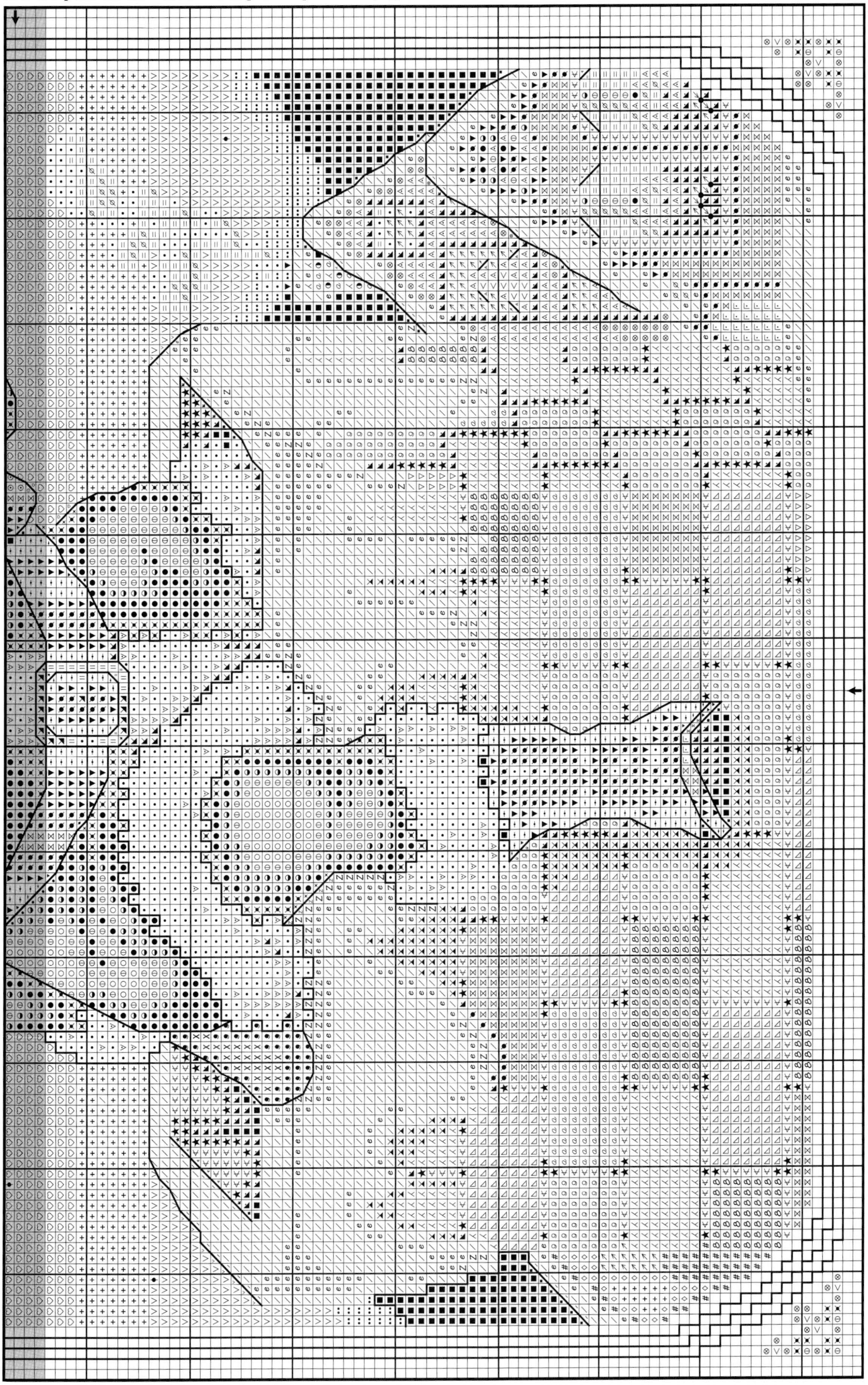

Heirloom Ornaments

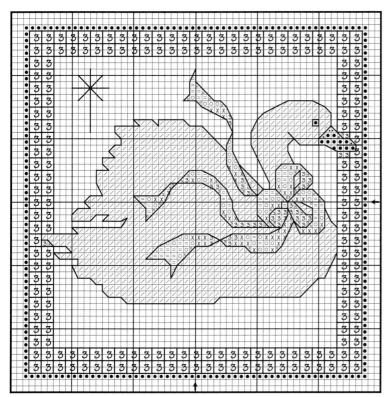

CHRISTMAS SWAN

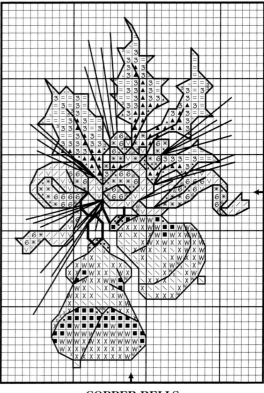

COPPER BELLS

CHRISTMAS SWAN

DMC Coats Anchor®

∕	white 1001	01	white
3	347 3013	13	salmon, dk.
X	3328 3071	10	salmon, med.
O	3712 3071	1023	salmon, med.
=	760 3069	894	salmon
●	783 5307	307	gold
	002HL Kreinik		gold
bs	498 3410	43	red, dk.

Fabric: 28-count evergreen linen from Wichelt Imports, Inc.
Stitch count: 56H x 56W
Design size:
25-count 4⅓" x 4⅓"
28-count 4" x 4"
30-count 3¾" x 3¾"
32-count 3⅓" x 3⅓"

Instructions: Cross stitch over two threads, using three strands of floss unless otherwise indicated. Cross stitch bow using two strands of floss. Backstitch using one strand of floss unless otherwise indicated. Straight stitch star using one strand 783/5307/307. Work rice stitches in border, using two strands 347/3013/13. When floss and Kreinik Metallics are bracketed together, use one strand floss and two strands Kreinik High Lustre Blending Filament.

Backstitch (bs) instructions:
498 3410 43 bow
783 5307 307 swan
002HL Kreinik

NOTE: See ornament finishing instructions, page 132.

COPPER BELLS

DMC Coats Anchor®

✳	814 3044	44	garnet, dk.
6	498 3410	43	red, dk.
V	347 3013	13	salmon, dk.
∕	3328 3071	10	salmon, med.
▲	500 6880	879	blue-green, vy. dk.
3	501 6878	878	blue-green, dk.
=	502 6876	877	blue-green
■	300 —	352	mahogany, vy. dk.
	052HL Kreinik		bronze
W	301 —	349	mahogany, med.
	021HL Kreinik		copper
X	3776 3336	349	mahogany, lt.
	021HL Kreinik		copper
⟍	402 —	347	mahogany, vy. lt.
	021HL Kreinik		copper
bs	3371 5478	382	black-brown

Fabric: 36-count sand Edinborough linen from Zweigart®
Stitch count: 46H x 31W
Design size:
25-count 3⅝" x 2⅓"
28-count 3¼" x 2¼"
32-count 2⅞" x 2"
36-count 2⅝" x 1¾"

(Continued on the next page)

Instructions: Cross stitch over two threads, using two strands of floss. Backstitch using one strand of floss unless otherwise indicated. Make straight stitches for pine needles, using one strand 500/6880/879. When floss and Kreinik Metallics are bracketed together, use one strand floss and two strands Kreinik High Lustre Blending Filament.

Backstitch (bs) instructions:

⌈ 300 — 352 rings on top of bells
⌊ 052HL Kreinik

3371 5478 382 remainder of back-stitching

NOTE: See ornament finishing instructions, page 132.

POINSETTIA AND HOLLY

DMC Coats Anchor®

✳	498	3410	43	red, dk.
W	347	3013	13	salmon, dk.
+	3328	3071	10	salmon, med.
╱	760	3069	894	salmon
■	890	6021	212	pistachio, ul. dk.
▲	319	6246	246	pistachio, vy. dk.
6	367	6018	210	pistachio, dk.
V	320	6017	215	pistachio, med.
C	368	6016	214	pistachio, lt.
–	369	6015	260	pistachio, vy. lt.
3	680	2876	907	old gold, dk.
L	729	2875	874	old gold, med.
‖	676	2874	887	old gold, lt.
o⌈	729	2875	874	old gold, med.
⌊	002BF Kreinik			gold
bs	3371	5478	382	black-brown

Mill Hill Glass Seed Beads

● 00367   garnet

Fabric: 25-count moss green Lugana® from Zweigart®
Stitch count: 50H x 50W
Design size:
25-count 4" x 4"
28-count 3⅝" x 3⅝"
30-count 3⅜" x 3⅜"
32-count 3⅛" x 3⅛"

Instructions: Cross stitch over two threads, using two strands of floss. Backstitch using one strand of floss unless otherwise indicated. Work eyelet stitches in center of each holly cluster, using two strands 347/3013/13. When floss color and Kreinik Metallics are bracketed together, use one strand floss and two strands Kreinik Blending Fila-

POINSETTIA AND HOLLY

CHRISTMAS TREE AND HEARTS

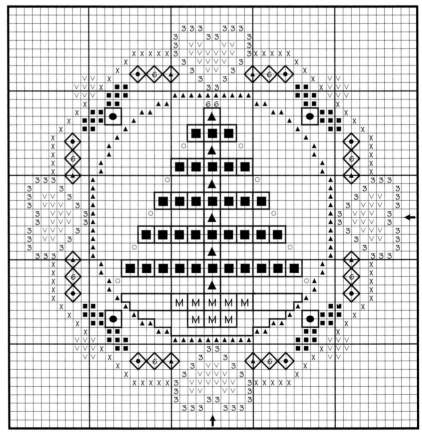

ment. Attach beads where ● appears at intersecting grid lines, using one strand 498/3410/43.

Backstitch (bs) instructions:
⌐729 2875 874 border between holly
└002BF
3371 5478 382 remainder of back-stitching

NOTE: See ornament finishing instructions, page 132.

CHRISTMAS TREE AND HEARTS

DMC Coats Anchor®
■	890	6021	212	pistachio, ul. dk.
▲	319	6246	246	pistachio, vy. dk.
3	321	3500	47	red
●	498	3410	43	red, dk.
M	420	5374	374	hazelnut, dk.
6	729	2875	874	old gold, med.
X	367	6018	210	pistachio, dk.
V	304	3401	19	red, med.
ss	368	6016	214	pistachio, lt.

Mill Hill Glass Seed Beads
○	02013		red, red

Fabric: 32-count cream Belfast linen from Zweigart®
Stitch count: 46H x46W
Design size:
25-count 3⅝" x 3⅝"
28-count 3¼" x 3¼"
30-count 3⅛" x 3⅛"
32-count 2⅞" x 2⅞"

Instructions: Cross stitch over two threads, using two strands of floss. Attach beads where symbol ○ appears, using one strand 304/3401/19.

Special instructions (See diagrams, page 132.):
1. Work eyelet stitches for Christmas tree and holly berries, using two strands of floss.
2. Work rice stitches for base of tree, using two strands 420/5374/374.
3. Work satin stitches (ss) below tree, using two strands 368/6016/214.
4. Work queen stitches on both sides of hearts, using two strands of floss.
5. Work four-sided stitches where symbol V appears in **middle of hearts only**, using two strands 304/3401/19.

NOTE: See ornament finishing instructions, page 132.

GIFTS FROM SANTA

DMC Coats Anchor®
⁄	white	1001	01	white
=	415	8398	398	pearl gray
V	414	8513	235	steel gray, dk.
▲	310	8403	403	black
+	841	5578	378	beige-brown, lt.
⁄⁄	842	5933	376	beige-brown, vy. lt.
✳	433	5471	944	brown, med.
M	435	5371	944	brown, vy. lt.
∪	437	5942	361	tan, lt.
◖	839	5360	360	beige-brown, dk.
↗	840	5379	379	beige-brown, med.
●	699	6228	923	green
X	701	6226	227	green, lt.
C	702	6239	239	kelly green
W	608	2332	332	orange
I	948	2331	778	peach flesh, vy. lt.
⊃	950	2336	376	flesh, lt.
–	761	3068	893	salmon, lt.
⌐	758	3868	868	terra cotta, lt.
⊙	760	3069	894	salmon
■	823	7982	150	navy, dk.
▼	336	7981	150	navy
○⌐	311	7980	148	navy, med.
└	002HL Kreinik			gold
·⌐	415	8398	398	pearl gray
└	001HL Kreinik			silver
⌐	744	2293	301	yellow, pl.
└	002HL Kreinik			gold
◣	824	7182	164	blue, vy. dk.
Z	825	7181	162	blue, dk.
∩	826	7180	161	blue, med.
3	680	2876	907	old gold, dk.
II	676	2874	887	old gold, lt.
··	743	2302	302	yellow, med.
○	321	3500	47	red
6	498	3410	43	red, dk.
✗	814	3044	44	garnet, dk.
N⌐	743	2302	302	yellow, med.
└	826	7180	161	blue, med.

Fabric: 27-count white Linda cloth from Zweigart®
Stitch count: 52H x 52W
Design size:
25-count 4⅛" x 4⅛"
27-count 3⅞" x 3⅞"
30-count 3⅓" x 3⅓"
32-count 3¼" x 3¼"

Instructions: Cross stitch over two threads, using two strands of floss. Backstitch using one strand of floss. Make French knots where ● appears at intersecting grid lines, using two strands
(Continued on the next page)

GIFTS FROM SANTA

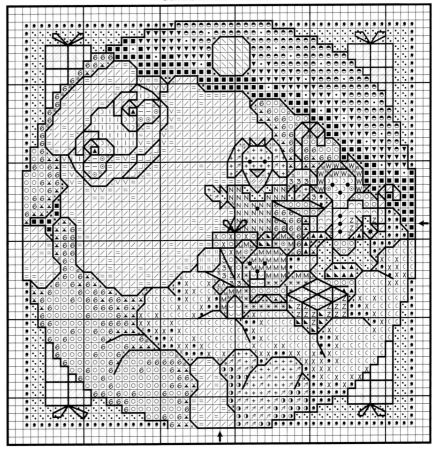

of floss and wrapping floss around needle once. Satin stitch using two strands of floss, making stitches in the direction of lines on chart. Make straight stitches using one strand of floss. Make lazy-daisy stitches using two strands of floss.

Backstitch instructions:

321	3500	47	stripes on candy canes
310	8403	403	pupils in Santa's eyes, horse's tail, horse's mane
839	5360	360	horse's bridle
680	2876	907	handle on horn
823	7982	150	remainder of backstitching

French knot instructions:

310	8403	403	bear's eyes, bear's nose, rabbit's eyes, horse's eyes
825	7181	162	buttons on rabbit's clothes, buttons on doll's clothes
760	3069	894	doll's nose

Satin stitch instructions:

321	3500	47	package in upper-left corner, package in lower-right corner
701	6226	227	package in upper-right corner, package in lower-left corner

Straight stitch instructions:

701	6226	227	ribbon on package in upper-left corner, ribbon on package in lower-right corner
321	3500	47	ribbon on checkerboard package in Santa's bag, ribbon on package in upper-right corner, ribbon on package in lower-left corner
702	6239	239	ribbon on solid red package in Santa's bag
498	3410	43	ribbon on solid blue package in Santa's bag

Lazy daisy instructions:

321	3500	47	bow on checkerboard package in Santa's bag, bow on package in upper-right corner, bow on package in lower-left corner
701	6226	227	bow on package in upper-left corner, bow on package in lower-right corner

NOTE: See ornament finishing instructions, page 132.

ELEGANT ANGEL

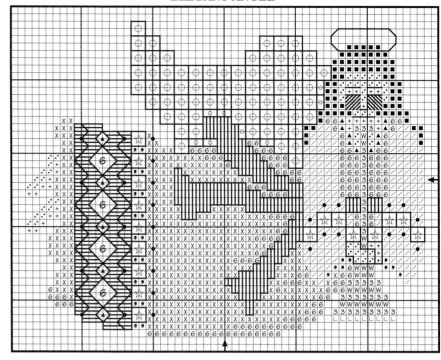

ELEGANT ANGEL

DMC Coats Anchor®

■	838	5831	380	beige-brown, vy. dk.
∴	948	2331	778	peach flesh, vy. lt.
+	950	2336	376	flesh, lt.
W	680	2876	907	old gold, dk.
3	729	2875	874	old gold, med.
L	676	2874	887	old gold, lt.
∕	ecru	1002	387	ecru
▲	500	6880	879	blue-green, vy. dk.
☆	501	6878	878	blue-green, dk.
	502	6876	877	blue-green
●	902	3083	897	garnet, vy. dk.
6	815	3000	22	garnet, med.
X	304	3401	19	red, med.
ss	758	3868	868	terra cotta, lt.
bs	840	5379	379	gold
O	284	Metallic Thread		gold

Mill Hill Glass Seed Beads
● 00557   gold

Fabric: 28-count antique tan linen from Wichelt Imports, Inc.
Stitch count: 43H x 56W
Design size:
25-count 3⅓" x 4⅓"
28-count 3⅛" x 4"
30-count 2⅞" x 3¾"
32-count 2⅝" x 3⅓"

Instructions: Cross stitch over two threads, using two strands of floss. Backstitch using one strand of floss. Attach beads where ● appears, using one strand 729/2875/874.

Backstitch (bs) instructions:
838   5381   380   eyebrows

304	3401	19	mouth
840	5379	379	eyes, chin, hands
284	Metallic Thread		halo

Special instructions (See stitch diagrams, page 132.):
1. Work Algerian eye stitches and partial Algerian eye stitches where symbol ○ appears in wings, using on strand 284 Metallic Thread.
2. Work diamond eyelet stitches where large diamonds appear on band of gown, using two strands 815/3000/22.
3. Work queen stitches where small diamonds appear on band of gown, using two strands 500/6880/879.
4. Work double cross stitch where symbol ▲ appears at neckline of gown, using two strands 500/6880/879.
5. Work rice stitches on right side of band of gown and on each sleeve, using two strands 501/6878/878 for bottom crosses and two strands 502/6876/877 for top crosses.
6. Work satin stitches (ss) using two strands of floss. Make stitches in the direction of lines on chart.

501	6878	878	lower sash, outer edges of band of gown
676	2874	887	around diamond eyelets and queen stitches on band of gown
500	6880	879	upper sash, sash at waist
502	6876	877	middle sash
758	3868	868	cheeks

NOTE: See ornament finishing instructions, page 132.

SLEIGH RIDE

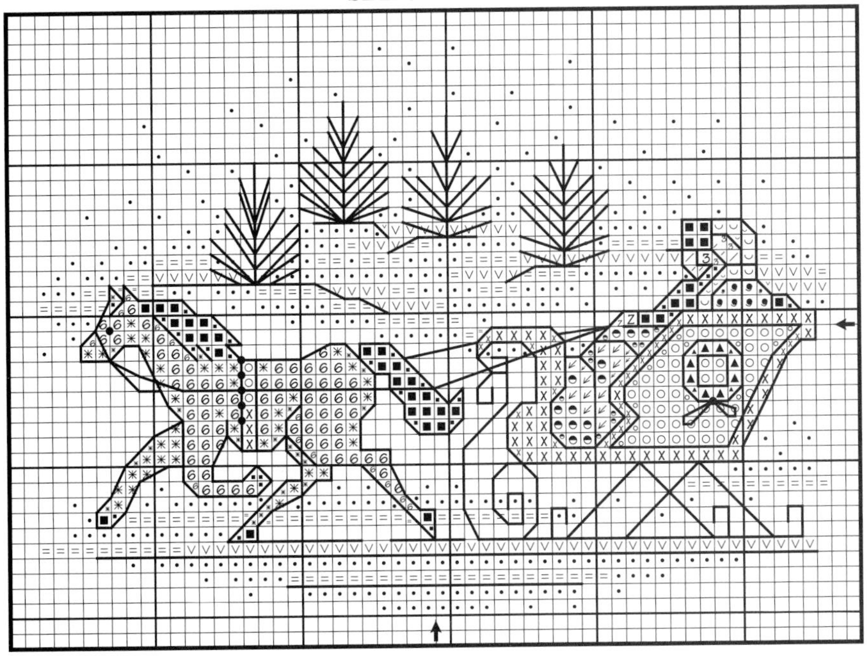

[chart image with grid]

SLEIGH RIDE

DMC Coats Anchor®

●	white 1001	01	white
=	⌈932 7050	343	antique blue, lt.
	⌊white 1001	01	white
V	⌈white 1001	01	white
	⌊931 7051	921	antique blue, med.
■	310 8403	403	black
*	838 5381	380	beige-brown, dk.
6	839 5360	360	beige-brown, dk.
▲	501 6878	878	blue-green, dk.
●	814 3044	44	garnet, dk.
X	816 3410	20	garnet
o	304 3401	19	red, med.
/	754 3146	6	peach flesh, lt.
3	433 5471	944	brown, med.
↙	⌈304 3401	19	red, med.
	⌊501 6878	878	blue-green, dk.
●	⌈816 3410	20	garnet
	⌊500 6880	879	blue-green, vy. dk.
∪	⌈613 —	956	drab brown, lt.
	⌊white 1001	01	white
Z	500 6880	879	blue-green, vy. dk.
Fk	729 2875	874	old gold, med.

Fabric: 28-count ice blue Annabelle from Zweigart®
Stitch count: 38H x 54W
Design size:
25-count 3" x 4⅜"
28-count 2¾" x 3⅞"
30-count 2⅓" x 3⅝"
32-count 2⅜" x 3⅜"

Instructions: Cross stitch over two threads, using two strands of floss. Backstitch using one strand of floss. Make French knots where ● appears at intersecting grid lines, using two strands of floss and wrapping floss around needle

once. Straight stitch using one strand of floss. Make lazy-daisy stitches for bow on wreath, using two strands 729/2875/874. When two colors are bracketed together, use one strand of each.

Backstitch instructions:
310 8403 403 horse, sleigh, people
500 6880 879 tree trunks

931 7051 921 lines in snow under sleigh and trees

French knot (Fk) instructions:
310 8403 403 horse's eye
729 2875 874 jingle bells on horse's harness, center of bow on wreath

Straight stitch instructions:
500 6880 879 pine tree branches
310 8403 403 halter and reins on horse (tack down to hold in place)

NOTE: See ornament finishing instructions, page 132.

THE HOLY FAMILY

DMC Coats Anchor®

⊙	754 3146	6	peach flesh, lt.
-	948 2331	778	peach flesh, vy. lt.
C	950 2336	376	flesh, lt.
▲	⌈895 6021	246	green, dk.
	⌊838 5381	380	beige-brown, vy. dk.
●	895 6021	246	green, dk.
*	3346 6258	268	hunter
■	838 5381	380	beige-brown, vy. dk.
⊖	839 5360	360	beige-brown, dk.

(Continued on the next page)

THE HOLY FAMILY

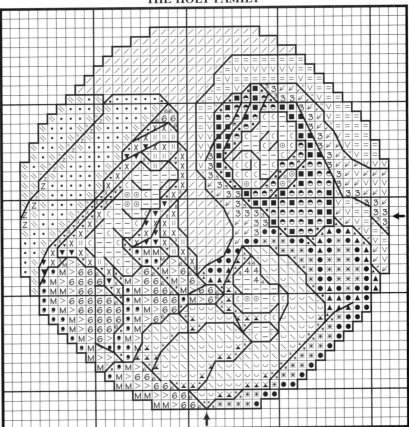

Symbol	DMC		Anchor	Color
▼	300	—	352	mahogany, vy. dk.
	838	5381	380	beige-brown, vy. dk.
X	300	—	352	mahogany, vy. dk.
II	400	5349	351	mahogany, dk.
=	739	5369	942	tan, ul. lt.
	white	1001	01	white
V	739	5369	942	tan, ul. lt.
∠	738	5375	372	tan, ul. lt.
3	437	5942	361	tan, lt.
4	436	5943	362	tan
◥	928	7225	274	gray-green, lt.
	white	1001	01	white
·	white	1001	01	white
Z	928	7225	274	gray-green, lt.
6	926	6007	850	gray-green, dk.
>	3768	6007	779	gray-green, dk.
M	924	6008	851	gray-green, vy. dk.
●	924	6008	851	gray-green, vy. dk.
	838	5381	380	beige-brown, vy. dk.
✗	640	5393	393	beige-gray, vy. dk.
∪	612	—	832	drab brown, med.
\	613	—	956	drab brown, lt.
∕	282 Metallic Thread			gold, lt. (**half cross**)
bs	3371	5478	382	black-brown

Fabric: 28-count blue wing linen from Wichelt Imports Inc.
Stitch count: 40H x 40W
Design size:
25-count 3¼" x 3¼"
28-count 2⅞" x 2⅞"
30-count 2⅝" x 2⅝"
32-count 2⅓" x 2⅓"

Instructions: Cross stitch over two threads, using two strands of floss unless otherwise indicated. Use one strand DMC Metallic Thread for half cross stitches. Backstitch using one strand 3371/5478/382. When two colors are bracketed together, use one strand of each.

Designed by Cathy Livingston

Ornament finishing instructions:
Complete cross stitch following instructions given. Cut backing fabric, allowing for seams. Place backing fabric and stitched front with right sides of fabric together. Hand or machine stitch around perimeter of design and zigzag close to first stitching to prevent raveling, leaving an opening for turning. Trim seams and turn. Stuff lightly with polyester filling. Whipstitch opening closed. Use floss, ribbon, or braid to form hanging loop, and tack at top, center of ornament.

Option: To trim edges of ornaments with decorative lace and/or piping that must be sewn into a seam, place trim between stitched front and backing pieces before sewing together, placing right side of trim against right side of ornament front and decorative edge of trim toward center of ornament.

ALGERIAN EYE

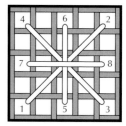
DOUBLE CROSS STITCH

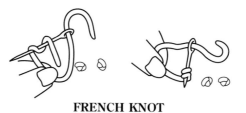

FRENCH KNOT **LAZY-DAISY STITCH**

 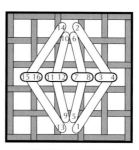 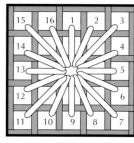
RICE STITCH **QUEEN STITCH** **EYELET STITCH**

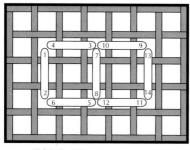 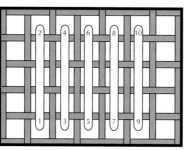
FOUR-SIDED STITCH **SATIN STITCH**

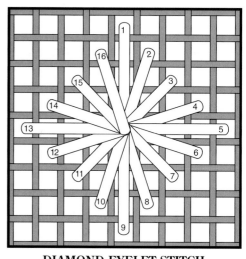
DIAMOND EYELET STITCH

Merry Christmas

Chart begins on page 134.

MERRY CHRISTMAS

DMC Coats Anchor®

	DMC	Coats	Anchor	
•	white 1001	01		white
⁄⁄	762	8510	397	pearl gray, vy. lt.
✕	413	8514	236	pewter gray, dk.
■	310	8403	403	black
X	666	3046	46	red, bt.
3	321	3500	47	red
N	304	3401	19	red, med.
◕	498	3410	43	red, dk.
●	890	6021	212	pistachio, ul. dk.
W	319	6246	246	pistachio, vy. dk.
6	367	6018	210	pistachio, dk.

	DMC	Coats	Anchor	
∧	320	6017	215	pistachio, med.
−	725	2298	305	topaz
⊙	783	5307	307	gold
G	741	2314	314	tangerine, med.
8	680	2876	907	old gold, dk.
↳	729	2875	874	old gold, med.
∪	353	3006	8	peach flesh
‖	948	2331	778	peach flesh, vy. lt.
⌐	470	6010	267	avocado, lt.
2	937	6268	268	avocado, med.
♥	791	7024	178	cornflower, vy. dk.
✶	792	7150	177	cornflower, dk.
≠	793	—	176	cornflower, med.
❘	794	—	175	cornflower, lt.

	DMC	Coats	Anchor	
◣	500	6880	879	blue green, vy. dk.
Z	501	6878	878	blue green, dk.
⁄	739	5379	942	tan, ul. lt.
=	738	5375	372	tan, vy. lt.
L	437	5942	361	tan, lt.
+	436	5943	362	tan
V	434	5000	379	brown, lt.
4	433	5471	944	brown, med.
◢	3371	5478	382	black-brown
M	838	5381	380	beige-brown, vy. dk.
>	839	5360	360	beige-brown, dk.
o	840	5379	379	beige-brown, med.
\	841	5578	378	beige-brown, lt.

Shaded portion indicates overlap from previous page.

Fabric: 25-count white Lugana® from Zweigart®; tray from Sudberry House

Stitch count: 95H x 184W

Design size:
14-count 6⅞" x 13⅛"
18-count 5¼" x 10¼"
25-count 7⅝" x 14¾"
27-count 7" x 13⅝"

Instructions: Cross stitch over two threads, using two strands of floss. Backstitch using one strand of floss un-

less otherwise indicated. Make French knots using two strands of floss, wrapping floss around needle twice.

Backstitch instructions:

890	6021	212	*Joy To The World, Noel* (two strands)
666	3046	46	ribbons on *Joy To The World* banner, both banners, both banner hangers (two strands)
937	6268	268	flower stems on shelf (two strands)
321	3500	47	nutcracker's teeth
3371	5478	382	remainder of back-stitching

French knot instructions:

321	3500	47	holly berries and berries on wreaths in border
783	5307	307	nutcracker's buttons
310	8403	403	Santa's buttons, all teddy bears' eyes, noses and belly buttons of bears in border

Designed by Cathy Livingston

God Bless America

Chart begins on page 138.

Happy Easter

Chart is on page 140.

GOD BLESS AMERICA

DMC Coats Anchor®

O	white 1001	01	white
Y	743 2302	302	yellow, med.
H	722 2323	323	spice, lt.
●	310 8403	403	black
W	433 5471	944	brown, med.
∵	948 2331	778	peach flesh, vy. lt.
△	839 5360	360	beige-brown, dk.
S	945 3335	881	flesh
▬	407 —	883	flesh, dk.
P	3716 —	25	dusty rose, vy. lt.
✎	3779 —	4146	terra cotta, ul. vy. lt.
⊗	758 3868	868	terra cotta, lt.
L	813 7161	160	blue, lt.
◑	3371 5478	382	black-brown
m	958 6186	187	sea green, dk.
\\	738 5375	372	tan, vy. lt.
X	798 7022	131	delft, dk.
Z	435 5371	363	brown, vy. lt.
ℓ	321 3500	47	red
◣	796 7100	133	royal blue, dk.
*	353 3006	8	peach flesh
C	334 7977	977	baby blue, med.
B	319 6246	246	pistachio, vy. dk.
‖	3347 6266	267	yellow-green, med.
6 ⎡	722 2323	326	spice, lt.
⎣	743 2302	302	yellow, med.
♡	352 3008	9	coral, lt.
bs	632 5936	936	coffee brown, dk.
bs	761 3068	893	light salmon
bs	962 3151	76	dusty rose, med.

Fabric: 27-count cream Linda® cloth from Zweigart®
Stitch count: 89H x 165W
Design size:
14-count 6¾" x 11⅞"
18-count 5" x 9¼"
25-count 7⅛" x 13¼"
27-count 6⅝" x 12¼"

Instructions: Cross stitch over two threads, using two strands of floss. Backstitch using one strand of floss unless otherwise indicated. Make French knots using two strands of floss, wrapping floss around needle once. When two colors are bracketed together, use one strand of each.

GOD BLESS AMERICA

Backstitch (bs) instructions:

3371	5478	382	moccasins, dress, and feathers on headband of Native-American girl, hands, face, nose, and mouth (two strands) of African-American boy
3347	6266	267	grass, flower stems
407	—	883	face and hands of Asian-American girl, cheeks of African-American boy
945	3335	881	face and hands of Caucasian boy
948	2331	778	face, hands, and cheeks of Caucasian girl
632	5936	936	face and hands of Native-American girl
310	8403	403	African-American boy's shoelaces
839	5360	360	nose and mouth of Native-American girl
758	3868	868	cheeks of Native-American girl
353	3006	8	cheeks of Asian American girl
3779	—	4146	cheeks of Caucasian boy
761	3068	893	nose, hands, and face of Caucasian girl and boy
962	3151	76	mouth of Caucasian girl and boy
352	3008	9	mouth and nose of Asian-American girl

French knot instructions:

435	5371	363	freckles on Caucasian girl
958	6186	187	beads on moccasins, headband, and dress of Native-American girl
743	2302	302	flowers

Designed by Charlotte Holder

FRENCH KNOT

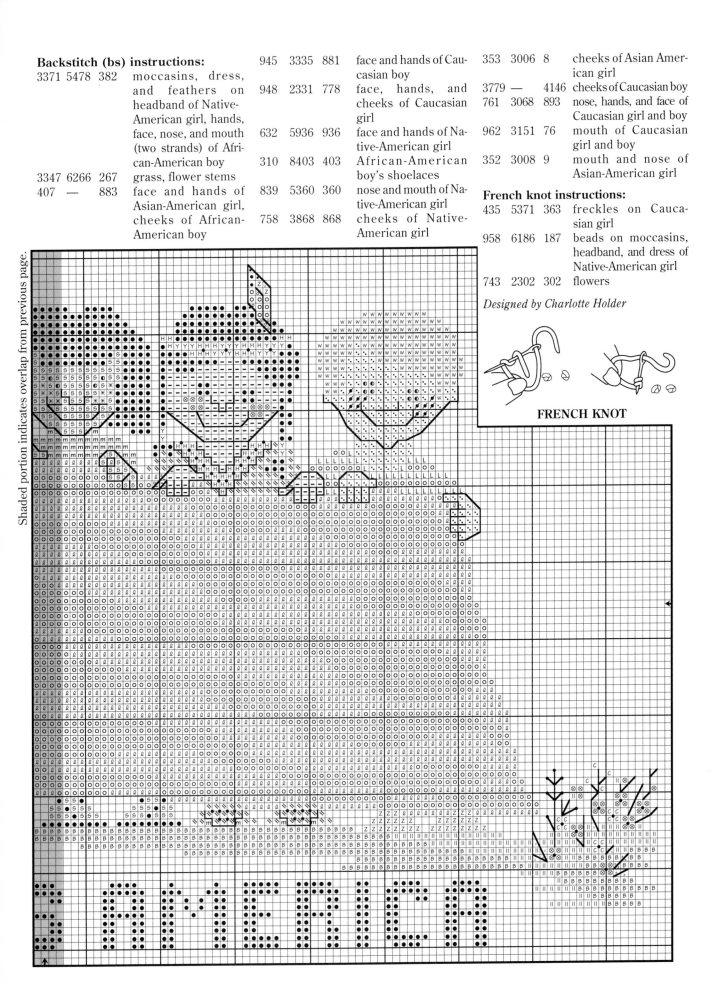

Shaded portion indicates overlap from previous page.

Shaded portion indicates overlap from above.

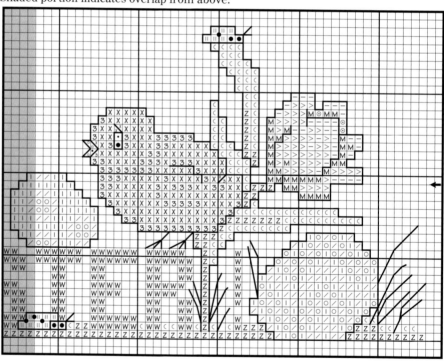

HAPPY EASTER

DMC Coats Anchor®

M	208	1002	111	ecru
>	209	4302	110	lavender, dk.
−	210	4303	108	lavender, med.
I	800	7021	144	delft, pl.
=	799	7030	130	delft, med.
+	956	3127	54	geranium
O	957	3125	52	green, pl.
∕	727	2289	293	topaz, vy. lt.
X	726	2295	295	topaz, lt.
3	725	2298	305	topaz
⊙	741	2314	314	tangerine, med.
●	3371	5478	382	black brown
·	white	1001	01	white
6	840	5379	379	beige-brown, med.
V	841	5376	378	beige-brown, lt.
\	842	5933	376	beige-brown, vy. lt.
C	3347	6266	267	yellow-green, med.
Z	3346	6258	268	hunter green
II	349	2335	13	coral, dk.
W	552	4092	101	violet, med.

Fabric: 27-count white Linda cloth from Zweigart®
Stitch count: 38W x 134H
Design size:
11-count 3½" x 12¼"
14-count 2¾" x 9½"
18-count 2¼" x 7½"
27-count 3" x 10"

Instructions: Cross stitch over two threads, using two strands of floss.

Backstitch using one strand of floss. Straight stitch using one strand of floss. Make French knots where ● appears at intersecting grid lines, using one strand 3371/5478/382 and wrapping floss around needle twice.

Backstitch instructions:
741 2314 314 chick's feet

3371 5478 382 remainder of back-stitching

Straight stitch instructions:
3347 6266 267 grass
840 5379 379 whiskers

French knot instructions:
3371 5478 382 spots on ladybugs

Designed by Cathy Livingston

Little Angel Ornament

DMC	Coats	Anchor®	Kreinik	
V	950	2336	376	flesh, lt.
=	352	3008	9	coral, lt.
6	351	3011	10	coral
W	312	7979	979	navy, lt.
O	322	7978	978	navy, vy. lt.
·	948	2331	778	peach flesh, vy. lt.
3	436	5943	362	tan
/			002C	gold cord (hs)
I	725	2298	305	028	topaz
X	783	5307	307	028	gold
bs	939	7160	152		navy, vy. dk.

Fabric: 25-count cream Lugana from Zweigart®

Stitch count: 28H x 28W

Design size:
14-count 2" x 2"
18-count 1½" x 1½"
25-count 2¼" x 2¼"
27-count 2⅛" x 2⅛"

Instructions: Cross stitch over two threads, using two strands of floss. Backstitch using one strand of floss unless otherwise indicated. Make half stitches (hs) in direction indicated by symbol, using one strand 002C. Make French knots for angel's eyes, using two strands 322/7978/978 and wrapping floss around needle twice. Make Smyrna cross stitches on skirt, using two strands Kreinik 028.

Backstitch (bs) instructions:
939 7160 152   angel, wings
            028 halo (two strands)

Designed by Cathy Livingston

FRENCH KNOT

SMYRNA CROSS

General Instructions for Cross Stitch

— •◦• —

Basic Supplies: Even-weave fabric, tapestry needle(s), six-strand embroidery floss, embroidery scissors, embroidery hoop (optional).

Fabric Preparation: The instructions and dimensions have been written and calculated for each of the projects shown stitched on the fabric listed in each color code. Alternate fabric choices have also been listed. If you wish to stitch a design on an alternate fabric, or alter its placement, you will need to recalculate the finished size of the project, as well as the yardage of materials needed, and make the necessary dimension adjustments.

Determine size of fabric needed for a project by dividing number of horizontal stitches by thread count of fabric. For example, if a design 35 stitches wide is worked on 14-count fabric, it will cover 2½" (35 divided by 14 equals 2½). Repeat process for vertical count. Add three inches on all sides of design area to find dimensions for cutting fabric. Whipstitch or zigzag edges to prevent fraying.

Floss Preparation: Cut floss into 14" to 18" lengths. Separate all six strands. Reunite number of strands needed and thread needle, leaving one floss end longer than the other.

Where to Start: Start wherever you like! Some designers suggest finding center of fabric and starting there. Others recommend beginning with a central motif, while still others work borders first. Many find fabric center, count up and back to the left, and start with the uppermost left stitch. Wherever you begin, be sure to leave allowance for all horizontal and vertical stitches so that a 3" fabric margin is left around completed design.

Should you choose to begin at the center point, find it by folding fabric from top to bottom and then from left to right. Use a straight pin to mark upper-left corner at junction of folds, and then unfold fabric. Pin will be in center of fabric.

After deciding where to begin on fabric, find same point on graph. Each square on graph represents one stitch. Those squares containing a symbol (i.e., X,T,O) indicate that a stitch should be made in that space over those threads. Different symbols represent different colors of floss for stitches. (See color code of chart.) They may also indicate partial or decorative stitches. Familiarize yourself with color code before you begin stitching. Even-weave fabric may be stretched over an embroidery hoop to facilitate stitching.

Stitching the Design: Using the diagrams on page 143, stitch design, completing all full and partial cross stitches first. Cross all full cross stitches in same direction to achieve a smooth surface appearance. Work backstitches second, and any decorative stitches last.

Helpful Hints for Stitching: Do not knot floss. Instead, catch end on back of work with first few stitches. As you stitch, pull floss through fabric "holes" with one stroke, not several short ones. The moment you feel resistance from floss, cease pulling. Consistent tension on floss results in a smoother look for stitches. Drop your needle frequently to allow floss to untwist. It twists naturally as you stitch and, as it gets shorter, must be allowed to untwist more often. To begin a new color on project, prepare floss and secure new strands as noted. To end stitching, run floss under several completed stitches and clip remaining strands close to surface. Many times it is necessary to skip a few spaces (threads) on the fabric in order to continue a row of stitches in the same color. If you must skip an area covering more than ¼", end stitching as described and begin again at next point. This procedure prevents uneven tension on the embroidery surface and snagging on back. It also keeps colors from showing through unstitched areas. Do not carry thread over an area that will remain unstitched.

When You Are Finished: For designs using cotton or linen floss on cotton or linen even-weave fabric, hand wash piece with mild detergent in warm water. Rinse thoroughly with cold water. Roll in terry towel and squeeze gently to remove excess moisture. Do not wring. Unroll towel and allow piece to dry until barely damp. Iron on padded surface with design face down, using medium setting for heat. A press cloth will help prevent shine on dark fabrics. **Note:** Acrylics, acrylic blends, wools or silks must be treated differently when cleaning. Check manufacturer's guidelines for special cleaning instructions.

Basic Stitch Diagrams

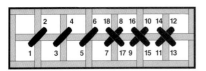

Full Cross Stitch (over one thread)

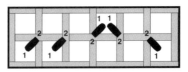

¼ Cross Stitch (over one thread)

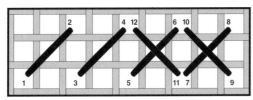

Full Cross Stitch (over two threads)

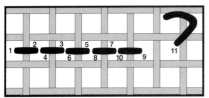

Basic Backstitch

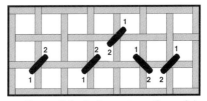

¼ Cross Stitch (over two threads)

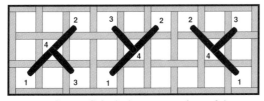

¾ Cross Stitch (over two threads)

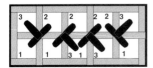

**¾ Cross Stitches
(over one in various
positions)**

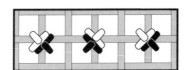

**Two ¾ Stitches
(in one square, using two
different floss colors)**

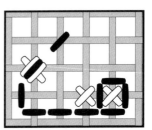

**Backstitch
(across two ¾ stitches
and around full cross)**

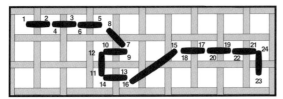

Backstitch (showing variations)

Shopper's Guide

Items not listed in "Shopper's Guide" are either commonly available, antiques, or from private collections.

Index

*Numbers in **bold** type indicate color photo pages.*
Numbers in regular type indicate chart and color-code pages.